Harshad Kotecha

Windows 7

4 Windows Explorer — 63

Windows Explorer	64
Computer Folder	65
Exploring Drives	66
Opening Windows Explorer	68
Navigation Pane	69
Libraries	70
Customize the Library	72
Address Bar	74
Customize Layout	76
Folder Contents	77
Changing Views	78
Sorting	79
Filtering	80
Grouping	81
Folder Options	82
Customizing Folders	84

5 Manage Files and Folders — 85

Select Files and Folders	86
Copy or Move Files or Folders	88
File Conflicts	92
Delete Files and Folders	94
The Recycle Bin	95
Create a File or Folder	98
Rename a File or Folder	99
Backtrack File Operations	100
File Properties	101
Open Files	102
Recent Items	103
Search for Files and Folders	104
Compressed Folders	105
Fonts Folder	107
Character Map	108

6 Working with Programs — 109

Start and Close Programs	110
Start Menu Searches	112
Create a Shortcut	113
Pin to Start Menu	114
Pin to Taskbar	115
Taskbar Grouping	116
Startup Folder	117
Minimized (or Maximized)	118
Install and Uninstall	119
Windows Features	120
Program Compatibility	121
Windows Virtual PC	122

Configure XP Mode   124
Command Prompt   126
Task Manager   128
Resource Monitor   130

7 Internet and Windows   131

Internet Connection   132
Start Internet Explorer   134
Browse the Web   136
Browser Buttons   138
Search the Internet   140
Change Search Provider   141
Bookmark Favorites   142
RSS Feeds   143
History   144
Home Page   145
Tabbed Browsing   146
Zoom   147
Print   148

8 Email and Messaging   149

Web Mail   150
Enable Pop Mail   152
Start Windows Live Mail   153
Receive Emails   155
Read a Message   156
Reply to a Message   157
Compose a New Message   158
Windows Live Contacts   159
Instant Messaging   160
Newsgroups   162
Block Spam Senders   164
Send a Web Page   166

9 Networking   167

Network Components   168
Set Up Your Network   169
Internet Connection   170
Discover Networks   172
Network and Sharing Center   173
Join the HomeGroup   174
Sharing a Printer   176
Network Map   177
View Network Components   178
Share Files and Folders   179
Network Troubleshooting   180

10   Customize Windows   181

Personalize Your Computer	182
Change Color and Sound	184
Screen Saver	186
Get More Themes	187
Windows 7 Basic	188
Desktop Icons	189
Screen Resolution	190
Display Settings	191
Desktop Gadgets	192
User Accounts	194
Configure the Account	196
Password Reset Disk	197
Date and Time Functions	198
Ease of Access Center	200
Mouse Settings	202

11   Digital Media   203

Upload Pictures	204
Windows Live Photo Gallery	206
Windows Live Movie Maker	208
Windows DVD Maker	210
Windows Media Player	212
Copy Audio CD	213
Play DVD Movies	214
Media Library	215
Online Resources	216
Windows Media Center	217

12   System and Security   219

System Properties	220
Performance Information	222
Clean Up Your Disk	223
Back Up and Recover Data	225
System Restore	226
Action Center	228
Windows Firewall	229
Malware Protection	230
Windows Update	231
Change Settings	232

Index   233

1 Introducing Windows

This chapter explains what Windows is and what's new in this latest version. It will help you identify the edition of Windows 7 that will suit you best, determine if your existing computer will handle Windows 7 and identify any actions needed. It also covers setup for the system and network, and using the mouse (or Windows touch facilities).

8   What is Windows?

9   Windows 7

10   Other Windows 7 Editions

11   Windows 7 Features

12   PC Requirements

13   32-Bit versus 64-Bit

14   Installation Options

15   Windows 7 Upgrade Advisor

16   Upgrade Reports

18   Starting Windows 7

20   Network Location

21   Finalize Settings

22   Windows Recovery

23   User Account Control

24   Using Your Mouse

25   Windows Touch

What is Windows?

Windows is an operating system for PCs (personal computers). The operating system is the software that organizes and controls all the components (hardware and software) in your computer so that they integrate and work efficiently together.

The first operating system from Microsoft was known as MS-DOS (Microsoft Disk Operating System). This was a non-graphical, line-oriented, command-driven operating system, able to run only one application at a time.

The original Windows system was an interface manager that ran on top of the MS-DOS system, providing a graphical user interface and using clever processor and memory management to allow it to run more than one application or function at a time.

Don't forget

There have also been versions of Windows aimed specifically at businesses, including Windows NT, Windows 2000, Windows 2003 and Windows 2008.

The basic element of Windows was its "windowing" capability. A window (with a lower-case w) is a rectangular area used to display information or to run a program. Several windows can be opened at the same time so that you can work with multiple applications. This provided a dramatic increase in productivity when using PCs, in comparison with the original MS-DOS.

Microsoft released four versions of this interface management Windows, with numerous intermediate versions, including:

- 1985 – Windows 1.0

- 1987 – Windows 2.0, 2.1 and 2.11

- 1990 – Windows 3.0, 3.1, 3.11 (Windows for Workgroups)

- 1995 – Windows 95, 98, 98 SE and Me (Millennium Edition)

The next version Windows XP was a full operating system in its own right. This was eventually followed by Windows Vista:

- 2001 – Windows XP (eXPerience) Home and Professional
- 2007 – Windows Vista Home, Home Premium, Ultimate etc

Hot tip

Windows XP and later versions no longer incorporate MS-DOS, though they do still feature a Command Prompt that permits DOS-like command line functions.

Windows 7

The latest version of Windows was released in 2009.

- **2009** – Windows 7 Starter, Home Premium, Ultimate etc

It is known as Windows 7, being the seventh major version (as Microsoft views the Windows product release cycle). It is based on the Windows Vista nucleus and displays the internal version number Windows 6.1. This sub-version numbering is intended to increase compatibility with existing applications that may be checking for Windows version 6.

Windows 7 is provided in several editions, aimed at different sections of the retail, business and emerging markets. Each edition includes all of the capabilities and features of the edition below it.

We'll start with the Windows 7 Retail editions:

Windows 7 Home Premium
This edition contains features aimed at the home market segment, such as Windows Media Center, Windows Aero and touch-screen controls. It provides an easy to manage environment for desktop, laptop and netbook computers.

Windows 7 Professional
This is targeted toward enthusiasts and small business users. It includes all the features of Windows 7 Home Premium, and adds the ability to participate in a Windows Server domain. It can also operate as a Remote Desktop server, and it supports features such as location aware printing, Encrypting File System and Presentation Mode.

Windows 7 Ultimate
This contains all the features of the Professional edition plus the business related features included in the Enterprise edition (see following page). Home Premium and Professional users can upgrade to the Ultimate edition for a fee using the Windows Anytime Upgrade (see page 14). Windows 7 Ultimate edition does not include the Ultimate Extras and other exclusive features that were incorporated into the Windows Vista Ultimate edition.

Other Windows 7 Editions

Windows 7 Starter

This is for beginner PC users who will make relatively limited use of their PCs. There are some particular exclusions: the Aero Glass transparency feature and related functions, the ability to personalize the system with your own theme or background, fast user switching allowing change of user without logging off, multimonitor support and DVD playback. All these are unavailable in the Starter edition. It does not offer a 64-bit variant. Early plans would have limited the system to running three applications simultaneously. However, this constraint has now been removed.

The Starter edition is available pre-installed on computers through system integrators or computer manufacturers (OEM system).

Windows 7 Home Basic

This is available in emerging markets including Brazil, People's Republic of China, India, Indonesia, Mexico, Pakistan, the Philippines and Thailand. It is not available in countries such as Australia, Canada, France, Germany, The Netherlands, Israel, New Zealand, the United States and the United Kingdom. Compared to the Premium edition, some Aero Glass options are excluded, and there are no games, no Windows Media Center and no support for Windows Multitouch. Like Starter, it is 32-bit only.

Windows 7 Enterprise

This is for the corporate or enterprise section. It has all the features of the Professional edition, plus support for Multilingual User Interface (MUI) packages, BitLocker Drive Encryption and UNIX applications. It includes a license to run multiple virtual machines and offers special activation facilities for volume users.

Windows 7 in Europe

Users in Europe can choose any edition of Windows 7 (except Home Basic) but will be given a browser ballot screen to select from a set of browsers (Internet Explorer 8 included).

Don't forget

Enterprise edition is not available as a packaged retail product or pre-installed on new PCs, but is provided only through volume licensing.

Beware

The competition law issues in Europe mean that proposals are subject to review and change, so you should check the latest position before making a European purchase of Windows 7.

Windows 7 Features

The editions of Windows 7 available to you may be constrained by the region in which you live, or by the way you obtain your copy of the product. However, you'll normally have a choice of edition, so it is useful to review the features that are available by edition:

Edition	S	HB	HP	Pro	Ent	Ult
Maximum memory (GB) [1]	4	4	16	192	192	192
HomeGroup	✓[2]	✓[2]	✓	✓	✓	✓
Desktop Window Manager	X	✓	✓	✓	✓	✓
Windows Mobility Center	X	✓	✓	✓	✓	✓
Windows Aero	X	✓[3]	✓	✓	✓	✓
64-bit	X	X	✓	✓	✓	✓
MultiTouch	X	X	✓	✓	✓	✓
Premium Games	X	X	✓	✓	✓	✓
Windows Media Center	X	X	✓	✓	✓	✓
Encrypting File System	X	X	X	✓	✓	✓
Location Aware Printing	X	X	X	✓	✓	✓
Remote Desktop Host	X	X	X	✓	✓	✓
Presentation Mode	X	X	X	✓	✓	✓
Windows Server domain	X	X	X	✓	✓	✓
Windows XP Mode	X	X	X	✓	✓	✓
AppLocker	X	X	X	X	✓	✓
BitLocker Drive Encryption	X	X	X	X	✓	✓
BranchCache Distributed Cache	X	X	X	X	✓	✓
DirectAccess	X	X	X	X	✓	✓
Subsystem for Unix Applications	X	X	X	X	✓	✓
Multilingual User Interface Pack	X	X	X	X	✓	✓
Virtual Hard Disk Booting	X	X	X	X	✓	✓

Note 1: 64-bit mode required for greater than 4 GB memory
Note 2: Join HomeGroup only, not create HomeGroup
Note 3: Partial support only for Windows Aero

As this table indicates, the Windows 7 editions are super sets of one another. Enterprise and Ultimate contain all the features of Professional, plus some exclusive features. Similarly, Professional includes all the features of Home Premium, plus extra features.

PC Requirements

The recommended specifications for PCs running Windows 7 are based on the processor mode used. On most current processors, you have the choice of 32-bit or 64-bit mode.

Windows 7 for 32-bit Processor Mode

The PC should have these minimum hardware requirements:

- Processor   1 GHz
- System Memory   1 GB
- Graphics   SVGA (800x600)
- Graphics adapter   DirectX9 class with WDDM 1.0 driver
- Graphics memory   128 MB (for Aero support)
- Hard Disk   16 GB available space
- Other   DVD-RW optical drive

Windows 7 for 64-bit Processor Mode

The PC should have these minimum hardware requirements:

- Processor   1 GHz
- System Memory   2 GB
- Graphics   SVGA (800x600)
- Graphics adapter   DirectX9 class with WDDM 1.0 driver
- Graphics memory   128 MB (for Aero support)
- Hard Disk   20 GB
- Other   DVD-RW optical drive

If you are planning to run Windows XP Mode on your Windows 7 system, the PC should have a minimum of 2 GB of memory and 15 GB of additional disk space. In addition, Windows Virtual PC requires a PC with Intel-VT or AMD-V enabled in the CPU, since the software relies on hardware virtualization features.

If you want to upgrade your existing PC to run Windows 7, you can run the Windows 7 Upgrade Advisor (see page 15) to identify any potential problems or short-comings.

32-Bit versus 64-Bit

As well as choosing your Windows 7 edition, you also need to decide between the 32-bit and the 64-bit versions of the operating system. This choice is available for all editions of Windows 7, except for Starter and Home Basic, with the retail packs including installation DVDs for each of these modes.

The 32-bit or 64-bit nomenclature refers to the memory address length which the processor can reference. This dictates the maximum amount of memory, which is 4 GB for 32-bit mode (or more exactly 3.4 GB, since some memory needs to be allocated to other purposes). For 64-bit mode, the maximum may be much higher, though the Windows 7 editions do not make full use of the potential. As well as more memory, 64-bit mode will also be faster, typically about 10%.

However, you need applications that are specifically optimized for 64-bit processing to take advantage of the speed improvements and memory increase. Many games for example include the necessary enhancements.

Remember that choosing a 64-bit system means that you can no longer run 16-bit applications. This is only a problem if you use very old software (from the Windows 3.1 days).

More seriously, existing 32-bit drivers for your devices will not operate in 64-bit mode, so you will have to locate 64-bit versions of the drivers. You may have problems with some devices, particularly the older ones.

You may also find that running 32-bit applications in a 64-bit operating system might actually be slower, due to the additional overheads imposed by conversion between the address systems.

In summary, if you have a 64-bit capable computer but use older hardware or 32-bit applications, you might do better to stay with the 32-bit version of Windows 7. With the latest hardware and drivers, and applications that are 64-bit optimized, especially demanding applications such as video editing or image packages, the switch to 64-bit and higher memory would offer significant improvements.

It won't be long before 64-bit computing becomes the standard, and 32-bit operation becomes an optional extra, but for the present there are still large numbers of 32-bit applications.

Beware

If your computer is more than a few years old, it is quite possible that you can only run the 32-bit version of Windows 7.

Don't forget

Applications such as Microsoft Office 2007 are still limited to 32-bit, although the follow-on version does include 64-bit support.

Installation Options

You can have Windows 7 installed onto your computer in several different ways:

- **Upgrade** – Replace an older version of Windows, retaining the installed applications and settings

- **Dual Boot** – Install Windows 7 while retaining the existing version of Windows, using a second disk partition. You'll need to install required applications to the new system

- **Clean Install** – Add Windows 7 to a newly formatted disk, then install all required applications

- **Pre-install** – Buy a new PC with Windows 7 already installed, then install the required applications

When you have an existing version of Windows on your PC, you can purchase an Upgrade version of Windows 7, which will be at a reduced price. However, you'll need to use the Dual Boot or Clean Install methods if the existing version of Windows is Windows XP, Windows 2000 or any version prior to these.

To illustrate the relative costs of the Upgrade and Full versions for the various editions of Windows 7, these are the prices in the United States:

Windows 7 Edition	Upgrade Price	Full Price
Home Premium	$119.99	$199.99
Professional	$199.99	$299.99
Ultimate	$219.99	$319.99

Microsoft also announced a Windows 7 Family pack. This contains three upgrade licenses for the Home Premium edition. It is being provided at a promotional price of $149.99.

If you already have Windows 7 on your computer, you can take advantage of the Windows Anytime Upgrade facility, to upgrade to a higher level edition. You can purchase the required product key from a store or online. You won't need a DVD or any downloads, since all the files required will already be included in your system. The upgrade will take only 10 or 15 minutes. Your current programs, files, and settings will be preserved.

Don't forget

To qualify for the Upgrade version of Windows 7 you must already have a version of Windows on your computer.

14

Windows 7 Upgrade Advisor

This checks your PC to see how well it could run Windows 7. It identifies known system or device compatibility issues, and suggests ways to resolve them.

 1 Go to the web page www.microsoft.com/window/windows-7/get/upgrade-advisor.aspx and click the button Download Windows 7 Upgrade Advisor

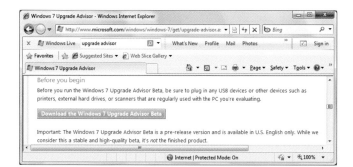

2 Follow the prompts to download and install the Upgrade Advisor

3 Run the Upgrade Advisor from the Start menu or desktop icon

4 Click Start Check to begin the analysis of your computer's hardware and software

Don't forget

Rather than type the whole address, you can go to the main www.microsoft.com website and search for Windows 7 Upgrade Advisor.

Hot tip

Each time you run the Upgrade Advisor, it will automatically update itself, so you get the latest changes.

Beware

Before you check your system, plug in any USB or other attachable peripheral that may be used on your PC.

15

Upgrade Reports

While the check takes place, you can visit the Windows 7 website to review features and compare the editions.

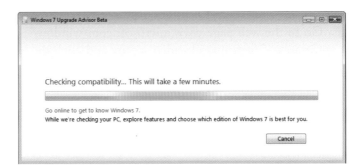

1 When Upgrade Advisor completes, it will advise you of the installation options available and any issues detected

2 Upgrade Advisor indicates that upgrade from Windows Vista Ultimate to Windows 7 Ultimate is allowed

3 Windows Mail, Parental Controls and Ultimate Extras are not included in Windows 7. There are no other issues with devices or programs detected on this computer

1 Run the Upgrade Advisor on a system with Windows XP, and you'll find that a full installation will be needed

Windows 7 Upgrade Advisor Beta

You need to prepare your system before installing Windows 7.   Save Report

System Requirements

⚠ **Upgrade**   Backup system first   You'll need to perform a custom installation of
                                                        Windows 7 and then reinstall your programs.
                                                        Make sure to back up your files before you
                                                        begin. Go online to get important information
                                                        about installing Windows 7.

✓ **Passed all 4 system requirements.**
   See all system requirements.

Devices

✓ **Intel(R) 537EP V9x DF PCI**   Action   Run Windows Update after installing Windows 7
   Modem   recommended   to make this device compatible.
   Intel Corporation

✓ **No issues detected.**
   See all devices.

Programs

✗ **Drive Image 7.0**   Reinstall with minor   You need to uninstall this program before
   version 7.03.402   issues   upgrading to Windows 7. You can reinstall this
   PowerQuest   version of the program, but you might
                                                      experience minor issues.
                                                      Visit the publisher's website.

⚠ **Tweak UI**   Minor issues   You might experience minor issues using this
                                                      program while running Windows 7. For more
                                                      information, go online to the manufacturer's
                                                      website.
                                                      Visit the publisher's website.

                                                      Start over   Close

2 In this example, the system resources on the Windows XP computer are sufficient to support Windows 7

3 The Upgrade Advisor warns you to run Windows Update (see page 231) after installing Windows 7, to make the Intel modem device compatible

The Upgrade Advisor identifies potential issues with the installed software even though you'll not be upgrading from Windows XP

1 Some software, for example Drive Image 7.0, must be uninstalled before Windows 7 upgrade, then re-installed

2 There may be minor issues using software designed for previous versions of Windows, though it will run under Windows 7.

Don't forget

Even when the computer fully meets the memory, processor and graphics card specifications, there may be additional needs, such as a TV tuner for media center operation.

Starting Windows 7

Whichever method of installing Windows 7 you have selected, you'll be asked to provide some appropriate details the first time you start up your system. For example:

 If requested, select the language and the country or region

2 When prompted, enter your username, amend the suggested computer name if desired, then click Next

3 Type a suitable password, re-enter it to confirm and then provide a hint to remind you of it, if you should forget

4 Enter the Product Key for your copy of Windows 7 – a combination of 5 sets of 5 letters and numbers

5 Use Recommended Settings, to allow Windows Update to maintain your system on a regular basis.

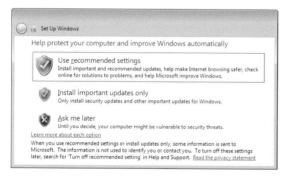

6 Check the date and time settings and adjust the Time Zone specified, if required

Network Location

If your computer is connected to a network, Ethernet or wireless for example, Windows 7 detects this and asks you to specify the type of network location involved.

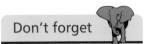
1 If prompted, choose an available wireless network from the list provided, and enter the appropriate security key

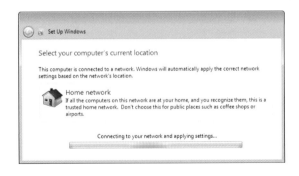

2 Choose Home, Office or Public depending on the location of your network

3 Windows will connect to your network and apply the necessary settings for the selected network location

If you select Home network, Windows will initiate the process for creating or joining a HomeGroup – a simple way to link computers on your home network together so that they can share pictures, music, videos, documents, and printers (see page 174).

Finalize Settings

 Windows finalizes the settings for your system

 Windows prepares your desktop using the revised settings for the Windows components in your system

The final stage in starting up your Windows 7 system for the first time is to log on to the user account specified during the installation.

 Finally, Windows makes your user account ready for use

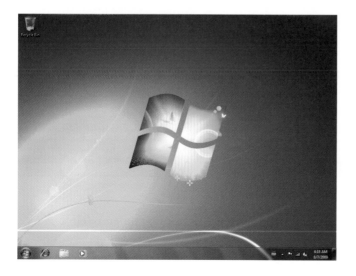

This illustrates the desktop with the default Windows 7 Aero theme. You can change this for an Aero theme with a slide show, or use your own pictures as background.

Windows Recovery

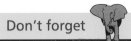

Don't forget

To view partition details, select Control Panel, System and Security, Administrative Tools. Double-click Computer Management, and select Disk Management.

When Windows 7 is installed as the only operating system on the hard drive, it creates a small separate System partition. On this partition it places the boot system files and access to a complete set of recovery tools, including Startup Repair, System Restore, Complete PC Restore and the Command Prompt.

To access the System Recovery Environment in Windows 7:

1 Start up the PC and, just before the system loads the Windows operating system, press the [F8] Function key

Hot tip

If there's no Recovery Partition on your system, you can boot from the Windows 7 installation DVD and select Repair Your Computer.

What to know before installing Windows

Repair your computer

2 On the Advanced Boot Options menu, select the Repair Your Computer option and press Enter

User Account Control

When you carry out tasks on your computer, you may be asked to grant permission to continue. This is due to User Account Control (UAC) which helps prevent unauthorized changes to your computer. UAC works by adjusting the permission level of your user account. If you're doing tasks that can be done as a standard user, such as reading email, listening to music, or creating documents, you have the permissions of a standard user – even if you're logged on as an administrator.

When changes to your computer that require administrator-level permission could be made, UAC notifies you.

For example, when signed on as an administrator:

 Click Start, type *regedit* and press Enter to run the Registry editor

 If you are signed on as an administrator, you just have to click Yes to continue

23

When signed on as a standard user, explicit permission is needed. For example, to make changes to user accounts:

Select Start, Control Panel and click Add or remove user accounts

The owner of the administrator-level account on the computer will have to enter the associated password for you to continue

Beware

When you get permission, you are temporarily given the rights of an administrator to complete the task and then your permissions are returned back to that of a standard user.

If there's more than one administrator account defined on the computer, you'll be able to select which one to use.

Using Your Mouse

The mouse is the usual pointing device used to communicate with your computer, it is an integral part of the user interface.

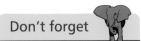

Right mouse button

Wheel

Left mouse button

LED (Light Emitting Diode)

The typical Windows mouse (like the Microsoft IntelliMouse Optical, shown above) includes the standard two buttons plus a wheel sited between them. Use your index finger to operate the small wheel. This provides an extra level of speed and control when scrolling up and down documents or even web pages – it's much faster than clicking on the scroll arrows displayed. You can even use the wheel to zoom into images and text.

To use a mouse, first place it on a flat surface or a mouse mat. You will notice an arrow-headed pointer (⬉) moving on your screen as you move the mouse.

To make a selection, move the mouse pointer on top of an item and then press and release (or click) the left mouse button. Sometimes you can click twice in rapid succession (double-click) to open a folder, window or a program.

A mouse will usually have at least one more button on the right (called the right mouse button). This provides additional facilities – for example, a click of the second mouse button (right-click) when it is over an appropriate object will display a shortcut menu of related options for further selection.

A mouse can also be used to move items on the screen. This is achieved by first moving the mouse pointer over an item. Then, press and hold down the left mouse button and move the mouse to position the item. Finally, once you see the item in the new location, release the mouse button. This technique is termed dragging.

We will be using the terms click, double-click, right-click and drag throughout this book, to refer to the mouse operations described above.

Windows Touch

Windows Touch provides another way to interact with the computer, if you have a touch sensitive screen or a tablet PC with multitouch capability, such as the HP TouchSmart TX2Z.

Hot tip

Other PCs supporting multitouch include the HP TouchSmart All-in-One PCs (IQ500 series & IQ800 series) and the Dell Latitude XT or XT2 Tablet PC.

With this, you can make single or multiple touches of the screen to indicate your requirements. For example, you'll be able to use natural gestures, to reach out and slowly scroll a web page then flick quickly to move through it more rapidly.

Applications that are touch optimized will take the fullest advantage of Windows Touch capabilities, but the gestures are designed to work with all applications, including those that were not specifically designed with touch in mind, by using default handlers that simulate the mouse or mouse wheel.

The touch and multitouch gestures supported in Windows 7 include the following:

Beware

Many screens and PCs can provide single touch functions. A single-touch PC will have the same functionality on Windows 7 as it has on Vista, but will not support full Windows 7 capabilities.

Thumbnail Peek

You can drag your finger across taskbar thumbnail previews and trigger a peek at the related window. A tap will switch to that window.

Show Desktop

The Show Desktop button supports a press-and-hold gesture that will expose your desktop temporarily, while a tap will clear down to the desktop (or restore the previously open windows).

Zoom in Windows Explorer

You can zoom in on an image by moving two fingers closer together, or zoom out by moving two fingers apart, for example to switch view modes from Small icons to Extra Large icons.

...cont'd

Multitouch Keyboard

With the soft touch keyboard you can press multiple buttons simultaneously, for example touch Shift+X to give a capital x.

Glow key feedback makes it clear which keys you are touching.

Context Menus

Touch an item with one finger and use another finger to tap, and you'll display the context menu (just as you do when you right-click with the mouse).

The following chart illustrates the range of gestures and actions that have been incorporated into Windows Touch.

Don't forget

The On-Screen keyboard can be found in the Ease of Access Center in the Control Panel, under Appearance and Personalization.

Hot tip

You may find other gestures incorporated into an application. For example, you could trace a question mark on the screen with your finger, and the application would respond by displaying a Help panel.

GESTURE	WINDOWS USAGE	GESTURE ACTION	ACTION (○= finger down | ◌= finger up)	Single Touch	Windows Touch
Tap / Double Tap	Click / Double Click			✓	✓
Panning with Inertia	Scrolling	Drag 1 or 2 fingers up and down			✓
Selection / Drag (left to right with one finger)	Mouse Drag / Selection	Drag one finger left / right		✓	✓
Press and Tap	Right-click	Press on target and tap using a second finger			✓
Zoom	Zoom (defaults to Control Scroll wheel)	Move two fingers apart / toward each other			✓
Rotate	No system default unless handled by Application (using WM_GESTURE API)	Move two fingers in opposing directions -or- Use one finger to pivot around another			✓
Two-Finger Tap	N/A – Exposed through Gesture API, used by Application discretion.	Tap two fingers at the same time (where the target is the midpoint between the fingers)			✓
Press and Hold	Right-click	Press, wait for blue ring animation to complete, then release		✓	✓
Flicks	Default: Pan up/ Pan Down/ Back, and Forward	Make quick drag gestures in the desired direction		✓	✓

2 Getting Started

In this chapter, the Desktop and Start menu are explained, and the Windows Live Essentials are introduced. Then the online help system is covered including how to get outside support if all else fails. Activation is discussed along with adding and using printers, then turning off or switching users.

28 Select User and Sign On

30 The Desktop

31 The Start Button

32 Getting Started/Welcome

33 Get Windows Live Essentials

35 Windows Live Settings

36 Antivirus Protection

38 Help and Support Center

40 More Support Options

41 Product Activation

42 Add a Printer

43 Print Preview

44 Turn Off Your Computer

46 Switch Users

Select User and Sign On

Each time you start up your computer, the Starting Windows image is displayed until the operating system has been loaded.

Starting Windows

When loading completes, the Welcome screen will be displayed to request your user sign on details.

1 If several user accounts are displayed, click your user name (or the associated picture)

Harshad

Harshad

Windows 7 Ultimate

2 If there's a password specified for this user account, type this, then press Enter (or click the arrow)

Harshad

3 If you mis-type the password, you get a warning message, and you must click OK to try again

Don't forget

You'll get an error message if you enter the wrong password or if you simply mis-key and cause an incorrect character to be added.

4 This time there will be a password hint as was specified when the user account was initially created

Harshad

Password

Password Hint: house number
Reset password...

5 Type the password correctly and press Enter

6 If you really have forgotten the password, and the hint isn't sufficient to remind you, you can select Reset password and enter a new password and password hint

Password Reset Wizard

Welcome to the Password Reset Wizard

If you forget the password for this user account and are unable to log on, this wizard helps you reset the password.

Note: To use this wizard, you must have first created a password reset disk.

To continue, click Next.

< Back   Next >   Cancel

Beware

To use password reset, you must have created a password reset disk (at a time when you did know the password). The disk can be a USB flash drive.

29

The Desktop

If you have a fresh installation (not upgraded from a previous version) your Windows 7 desktop should not have any icons except the Recycle Bin. However, you can display standard icons (see page 189) or add your own shortcut icons (see page 113).

(see page 189) (see page 113)

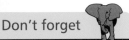

Don't forget

Your actual desktop layout depends on the Windows components and software you have installed, any customizing that has been done and whether the active theme is Aero or Basic (see page 188).

(see page 188)

Don't forget

Unlike Vista, there is no Welcome Center or Sidebar displayed when you start up, though you can add gadgets to the desktop (see page 192). There's also no Quick Launch Bar, but there is an enhanced Taskbar which features program launch buttons.

(see page 192)

Hot tip

Just in case there are too many tasks to fit on the Taskbar, Windows by default will group like items together. These are shown as overlapped buttons.

30

The desktop displays in this example an Aero Themes landscape image. At the bottom, you'll find the Taskbar, with the Start button (sometimes called Start Orb) and program launch buttons, and to the right the Notification Area with system icons.

Move the mouse pointer over the Start button and it brightens to show that it is active. Click the Start button to select your programs and files, change settings, get help and support or logoff and shutdown.

The Taskbar has launch buttons for Internet Explorer, Windows Explorer and Windows Media Player. It also has buttons for all the active programs and open windows.

The notification area has speaker, network and other system icons, and at the far right the Aero Peek/Show desktop button.

The Start Button

1 Click the Start button (or press the Windows Logo key on its own) to display the Start menu, from where you start programs, access files, customize settings and so on

Hot tip

You won't find entries such as the Internet Browser at the top of the Start menu. These have been moved to the Taskbar.

Don't forget

The entries on the left are likely to change, since they are shortcuts to programs you have recently used or installed.

31

The Start button provides access to all activities that you might require, but the main display has a subset that includes most recently used programs and recently installed programs, these being items that you're likely to want to work with

2 Click the down arrow next to a program, to list recently opened items

Don't forget

Place your mouse pointer over All Programs to access all your installed programs or begin typing the program name in the Start menu Search field (see page 112).

On the right you'll see the user account picture and the user name, plus the main folders and functions. Windows 7 uses the terms Documents, Pictures and Music introduced in Windows Vista to replace My Documents, My Pictures etc. However, these terms now refer to Libraries, which include files of the relevant type that are stored in multiple locations on your system.

Getting Started/Welcome

32

Don't forget

The Getting Started option has similar functions to those offered by the Welcome Center featured in Windows Vista.

Hot tip

If Getting Started is not on the Recently Used section of the Start menu, you can find it by selecting Start, All Programs, Accessories.

Hot tip

Hover the mouse over the Getting Started entry and after a moment the list of tasks will appear.

 Click Start and select the Getting Started link to display a set of useful tasks for setting up your system

2 Click a task to see a more detailed description, then click the activation link (or double-click the task) to start it

Alternatively, to display a menu list of the tasks:

1 Click Start, then click the Getting Started down arrow

2 Click one of the tasks e.g. Personalize Windows, to run it

Get Windows Live Essentials

1 Select Getting Started and click the option to Get Windows Live Essentials

Hot tip

Windows Live Essentials are free programs for online communications, photo editing and security. They include applications that are in previous versions of Windows but excluded from Windows 7:
 Windows Mail
 Windows Movie Maker
 Windows Photo Gallery

2 Select your language and click Download

3 If prompted, click Run for the Windows Live setup program

33

Don't forget

Select a program name to see a description of that program and a list of the applications and utilities that will be installed along with it. The totals show the disk space needed and the disk space available on your drive.

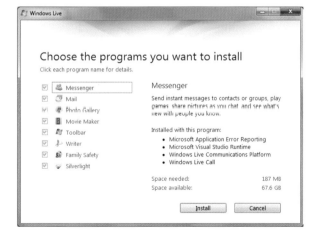

4 Click the boxes to select or deselect the programs you want, then click the Install button

...cont'd

5 Windows Live checks for open programs and warns you if any need to be closed, for example Internet Explorer

Beware

Windows Live setup will need to update the files for some programs. Save your work and close these programs then click Refresh.

6 When all required data has been saved, click Continue to start the download of all the applications and utilities

Don't forget

Each program is downloaded and installed in turn, and as this proceeds, useful information about Windows Live services will be displayed.

Windows Live Settings

1 When download and installation completes, you are asked to select your settings for search provider and home page

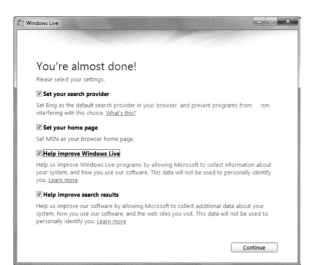

Hot tip

You can also allow Microsoft to collect information about your system and how you use the Windows Live programs and search facilities. This will not personally identify you.

2 Click Continue, and you are given the opportunity to sign up for a Windows Live ID

3 Select Start, All Programs, Windows Live to see the list of programs that are added to your system and Start menu

Don't forget

Windows Live ID is a single sign in for Windows Live Messenger, MSN Hotmail, MSN Music, and other sites and services. If you don't want to sign up at this point, you will be able to sign up later from Windows Live Messenger (see page 160).

Antivirus Protection

Another application that's missing from Windows 7 (and previous versions of Windows) is Antivirus Protection. Windows itself points this out, with a warning message in the Action Center.

1 Move the mouse pointer over the Flag icon in the notification area to see the message count

2 Left-click the icon for brief details of the message(s), then click Open Action Center

3 The message is the warning that Windows did not find antivirus software on the computer

4 Click the button to Find a program online to display the Windows 7 Security software providers

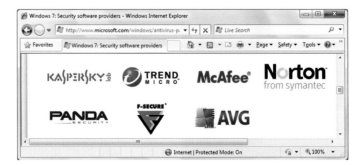

36

5 Select the company name to see the products that they offer for Windows 7, e.g. click AVG

6 You can purchase AVG Anti-Virus or the full AVG Internet Security product, or download trial versions

7 If it will be for private use only, you can download the AVG Anti-Virus Free Edition from http:/free.avg.com/

8 Click Get It Now, and follow the prompts to download and install the AVG software

Help and Support Center

1 Click Start and then click the Help and Support button or press the F1 key from the desktop

2 Select one of the general starting points, for example Learn about Windows basics

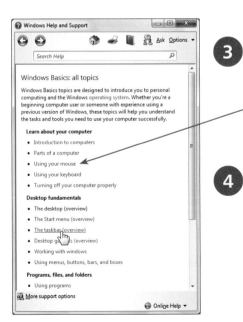

3 You'll see an organized list of topics and sub-topics, for example Learn about your computer, and under this Using your mouse

4 To illustrate, click the sub-topic title The taskbar (overview), found under the topic heading Desktop fundamentals

When you select a sub-topic, an article is displayed with links to sections within the document.

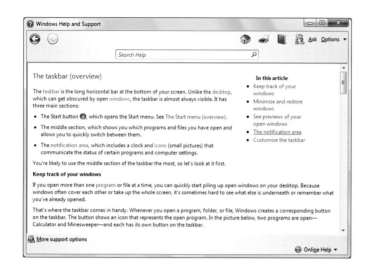

Hot tip

When your computer is connected to the Internet, your searches can include the latest Help content from the Online website. Click the Online Help button to check if this is enabled.

5 Click a link such as The notification area, to move to another section of the Help article

Don't forget

Click the Back and the Forward buttons to review previously viewed portions of the help information.

If you don't find the topic you're looking for in the topics or contents list, use Search Help.

1 From any Help and Support Center panel click the Search Help box, type a word or phrase, then press Enter (or click the Spy glass) to list matching entries

More Support Options

 Click the Ask button on the toolbar (or click More Support Options at the foot of the Help window) for additional sources of help

Hot tip

You can ask a friend, consult a volunteer, contact technical support or search for solutions to your question on one of the Windows websites.

Hot tip

It's possible that your friend or work colleague has encountered the same problems as you've been experiencing. Therefore, with your permission, they can access your system and see your desktop in the hope that they'll be able to help.

 Click Windows Remote Assistance and click the option to Invite someone you trust to help you

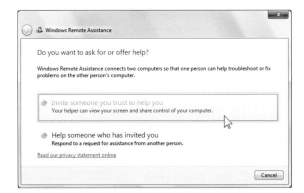

Beware

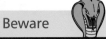

You must only share control of your system with an individual or company you really trust.

You can send the invitation by email. However, if you use web based email, you should save it as a file that you attach to a message to your helper

Product Activation

You'll have 30 days to activate Windows 7 after installing it. To check the current status:

 1 Select Start, type *System*, select the System option from the list then scroll down to the Windows activation section

2 If Windows 7 is awaiting activation, click the link, then click Activate Windows online now

3 When activation completes, you'll be told that your copy of Windows 7 has now been validated as genuine

4 The status in the System panel will be updated

Hot tip

The purpose of Product Activation is to reduce software piracy and to ensure that a licensed copy is used on one PC.

Hot tip

Activation takes under a minute to complete over the Internet and no personal details are collected. If you don't have Internet access you can choose to complete the activation over the phone.

41

Don't forget

If your copy of Windows 7 was pre-installed by the computer supplier, activation may already have been carried out on your behalf.

Add a Printer

In most cases Windows will automatically install the software that will allow it to work on your computer. To add a local printer, directly attached to your computer:

 Connect the printer to the computer and switch the printer on (note: for parallel cable connections, you should shut down the computer before you attach the printer)

 Restart the computer, if required, and Windows will automatically detect the printer and start adding software

3 After a few moments, Windows should tell you that the device is installed and ready for use

4 To check the printer definition, select Start, Control Panel and select the Devices and Printers link

Print Preview

1 Click the arrow on the application button, in this case the WordPad button, and select Print, Print Preview

Don't forget

You can see what the print copy of your document will look like, without actually printing it to paper, if the application you are using offers the print preview function.

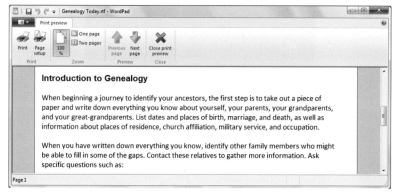

Introduction to Genealogy

When beginning a journey to identify your ancestors, the first step is to take out a piece of paper and write down everything you know about yourself, your parents, your grandparents, and your great-grandparents. List dates and places of birth, marriage, and death, as well as information about places of residence, church affiliation, military service, and occupation.

When you have written down everything you know, identify other family members who might be able to fill in some of the gaps. Contact these relatives to gather more information. Ask specific questions such as:

2 You can view all the pages one or two at a time, or zoom in to view the document at 100% size

3 Click the Page Setup button from Print Preview (or select Page setup from the application menu) to change the document layout

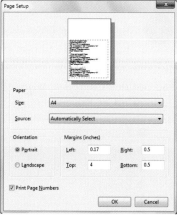

4 Click OK to apply the changes, then click the Print button from Print Preview (or select Print from the application menu)

Turn Off Your Computer

Don't forget

In Windows 7 Shutdown is the default option for the Power button, unlike Windows Vista which had the default set to Sleep mode.

To shut down your computer:

1 Select Start then click the on-screen Power button, to start shutting down Windows

2 If open files need to be saved, Windows warns you

3 After a few moments, if you take no action (or the program doesn't close), Windows offers Force shut down

Hot tip

Sometimes, you may see a warning flag (!) in the Power button, to indicate that updates to Windows will be applied before the computer shuts down.

1 program still needs to close:

(Waiting for) Untitled - Notepad
This program is preventing Windows from shutting down.

To close the program that is preventing Windows from shutting down, click Cancel, and then close the program.

Force shut down   Cancel

4 When all active programs are closed (or you choose forced shut down) Windows logs off, shuts down and the computer powers off

You can select a different action when appropriate.

1 Select Start, then click the arrow next to the Power button, and choose the desired option

The options offered may include some or all of the following:

- Switch User
- Log off
- Lock
- Restart
- Sleep
- Hibernate

Beware

Depending on the hardware features of your computer, some of these options may be missing or greyed (inactive).

44

You can change the default action for the on-screen Power button

 1 Right-click the on-screen Power button and select Properties

 2 Choose your preferred option and click OK

 3 The new option appears on the Power button

You can also specify the action to be taken when you press the hardware Power button.

 1 Select Start, Control Panel, Hardware and Sound to view Power Options. These vary between laptops and desktops

Power Options
Change battery settings
Change what the power buttons do
Require a password when the computer wakes
Change when the computer sleeps
Adjust screen brightness

Power Options
Change battery settings
Change what the power buttons do
Require a password when the computer wakes
Change when the computer sleeps
Adjust screen brightness

45

 2 You can select the action to carry out when you press Power (or Sleep or close the lid for a laptop)

Define power buttons and turn on password protection
Choose the power settings that you want for your computer. The changes you make to the settings on this page apply to all of your power plans.

Power and sleep buttons and lid settings

	On battery	Plugged in
When I press the power button:	Sleep	Sleep
When I press the sleep button:	Sleep	Sleep
When I close the lid:	Sleep	Sleep

Do nothing
Sleep
Hibernate
Shut down

Password protection on wakeup
○ Require a password (recommended)
When your computer wakes from sleep, no one can access your data without entering the correct password to unlock the computer. Create or change your user account password
○ Don't require a password
When your computer wakes from sleep, anyone can access your data because the computer isn't locked.

Save changes   Cancel

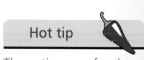

Switch Users

If you have a number of user accounts defined on the computer, several accounts can be active at the same time – you don't need to close your programs and log off to be able to switch to another user and it's easy to switch back and forth.

Don't forget

All your settings and files are maintained but the new user won't be able to see them; and you won't be able to see theirs when you switch back. Your screen will look exactly the same as you left it.

Hot tip

You can have two or more user accounts logged on, and use either of these techniques to switch between these users.

Beware

If the other accounts have data files open, shutting down without logging them off could cause them to lose information.

 Click the Start button, click the down arrow next to the Shut down button, and select the Switch User option

 You may now allow another user to select their account, or let a visitor select the Guest account

As an alternative way to switch users:

 Press Windows logo key + L, to lock the current user

Press the Switch User button on the logon panel and select another account, as shown above

Shut Down

When you turn off your computer (see page 44), you'll be warned if there are other user accounts still logged on to the computer.

Click Yes to shut down anyway, or click No, to allow the other accounts to log off individually

3 Basic Controls

Most of what you do in Windows 7 will be done using a menu, dialog box or a window. This chapter shows you how you can use these structures, and in particular how you control and manage all the windows used for files, folders and programs.

48	Menus
49	Dialog Boxes
50	Structure of a Window
51	Moving a Window
52	Restoring a Window
53	Resizing a Window
54	Arranging Windows
56	Aero Snaps
58	Switching Windows
59	Windows Flip and Flip 3D
60	Arranging Icons
61	Scrolling
62	Closing a Window

Menus

Traditionally, windows have a Menu bar near the top, displaying the menu options relevant to that particular window. Simply click on a menu option to reveal a drop-down list of further options.

 Select Start, Documents to display the folder window

 Click View to display the View menu

A bullet shows an option to be active but only one option can be selected from a group. Clicking another option from the group will automatically turn off the previously selected one.

The forward arrow indicates that there is another linked menu for selection. Move the mouse arrow onto the option to see it.

Hot tip

The ellipse (i.e. ...) indicates that if this option is selected, an associated window with further selections will be displayed.

A tick shows that an option is active. To deactivate an option with a tick next to it, click on it. Click on it again to activate it.

Hot tip

If an option is greyed (dimmed out), it is not available for use at this particular time or is not appropriate.

Some options may have shortcut keys next to them (e.g. Alt+Up arrow – Up one level), so you can use these instead of clicking on the entries with your mouse. Other examples of shortcut keys are:

Ctrl+A – Select All	Ctrl+C – Copy	Ctrl+V – Paste
Ctrl+X – Cut	Ctrl+Y – Redo	Ctrl+Z – Undo

The menu bar continues to be used for applications such as Notepad and Calculator. However, it has been replaced by the new Scenic Ribbon (see page 50) in Windows applications such as WordPad and Paint.

48

Dialog Boxes

Although simple settings can be made quickly from menu options, other settings need to be made from windows displayed specifically for this purpose. These are called dialog boxes.

Tabs

Some dialog boxes are divided into two or more tabs (sets of options). Only one tab can be viewed at a time.

Check Boxes

Click on as many as required. A tick indicates that the option is active. If you click it again it will be turned off. If an option is greyed, it is unavailable and you cannot select it.

Radio Buttons

Only one out of a group of radio buttons can be selected. If you click on another radio button, the previously selected one is automatically turned off.

Command Buttons

OK will save the settings selected and close the dialog box or window. Cancel will close, discarding any amended settings. Apply will save the settings selected so far but will not close, enabling you to make further changes.

Spin Boxes

Spin boxes let you type or select numbers only. They usually have arrow buttons to allow you to increment or decrement the values.

Hot tip

These examples are from the Folder Options dialog box. Select Tools, Folder options from the Menu bar, or Organize, Folder and Search Options from the Command bar.

Don't forget

You can select the option to Always show menus, and the menu bar will display permanently in folder windows.

49

Hot tip

These spin boxes are from the Taskbar and Start Menu Properties dialog box.

Structure of a Window

You can have a window containing icons for further selection or a window that displays a screen from a program. All these windows are similar in their structure, though Windows 7 does add some features which do not yet appear in all Windows applications.

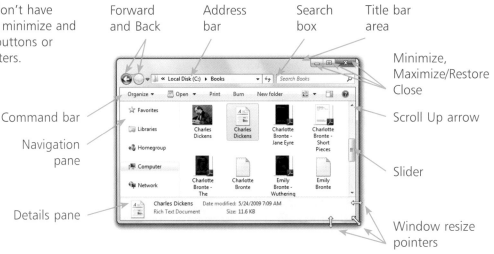

Forward and Back | Address bar | Search box | Title bar area

Minimize, Maximize/Restore Close

Command bar

Navigation pane

Details pane

Scroll Up arrow

Slider

Window resize pointers

Scroll bars will only appear when there are items that cannot fit into the current size of the window. Here only a vertical scroll bar is needed.

If you move the mouse pointer over any edge of a window, the pointer changes shape and becomes a double-headed resize pointer – drag it to change the size of a window (see page 53).

Double-click on an icon to open a window relating to it, in this case a WordPad application window. This window has Quick Access toolbar, Menu bar, Scenic Ribbon, Ruler, two Scroll bars, a title in the Title bar area and a Control icon at the top left.

Moving a Window

As long as a window is not maximized, i.e. occupying the whole screen, you can move it. This is especially useful if you have several windows open and need to organize your desktop.

1 Move the mouse pointer over the Title bar of a window

2 Drag the mouse pointer across the desktop (left-click and hold the mouse button down as you move)

3 When the window reaches the desired location, release the mouse button to relocate the window there

Control Menu Move

There's a Move command for the window on the Control menu.

1 Right-click the Title bar and select Move, and the mouse pointer changes to a four headed arrow

2 Click on the window, holding down the left mouse button and moving the pointer towards the Title bar

3 The mouse pointer changes to an arrow, grabs the window and you can move and drop it as above

Don't forget

You will see the whole window move, with the full contents displayed, and transparency still active, while you are dragging the window.

Hot tip

If you have two monitors attached to your system, you can extend your desktop onto the second monitor and drag a window from one monitor onto the other.

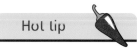
Hot tip

If the Title bar has a Control icon, left-click this to show the menu.

51

Restoring a Window

Hot tip

You can also double-click the Title bar to Maximize the window. Double-click again to Restore it to the original size.

A window can be maximized to fill the whole screen, minimized to a button on the Taskbar or restored to the original size.

Original size window　　Maximize button　　Maximized window

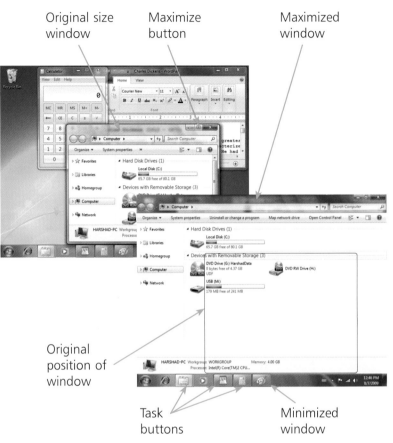

Hot tip

You can also use Aero Snaps to maximize, move or resize windows (see page 56).

Original position of window

Task buttons　　　Minimized window

Whether a window is maximized or original size, click on the minimize button (left of the top-right three buttons) to reduce the window to its Task button. This will create space on the desktop for you to work in other windows. When you want to restore the reduced window, simply click its Taskbar button.

Don't forget

You can right-click the Title bar area or left-click the Control icon, to display the Control menu (see page 51).

The middle button is the maximize button or – if the window is already maximized – the button changes to the restore button.

Click Close, the third button, when you want to end a program or to close a window.

Resizing a Window

If a window is not maximized or minimized, it can be resized.

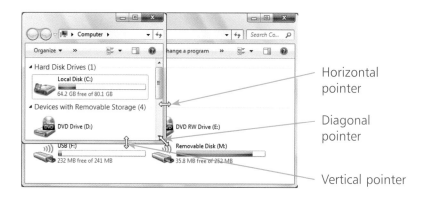

Horizontal pointer

Diagonal pointer

Vertical pointer

Hot tip

Resize and move all the windows on your desktop to organize the layout to the way you prefer to work, or see page 54 for other ways of arranging windows.

1 Place the mouse arrow anywhere on the edge of a window or on any of the corners. The pointer will change to a double-headed resize pointer

2 Click and drag the pointer outwards to increase the size of the window or inwards to reduce the size. Release the mouse button when the window is the desired size

Control Menu Size

There's a Size command on the Control menu which makes it easier to grab the edge of the window.

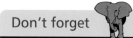

Don't forget

Some windows are fixed and cannot be resized. These include dialog boxes and applications, such as the Windows Calculator.

1 Right-click the Title bar (or left-click the Control icon) and select Size

2 The mouse pointer changes to a four headed arrow

3 Click the window, holding down the left mouse button, and move the pointer towards an edge or a corner of the window

4 The mouse pointer changes to a double-headed arrow and grabs the edge or corner, so you can stretch the window to the desired size, then release the mouse button

53

Arranging Windows

If you have several windows open on your desktop and you want to automatically rearrange them neatly, rather than resize and move each one individually, use the Cascade or Tile options.

1 Right-click a clear area on the Taskbar to display a shortcut menu and select one of the three arrangement options

2 Cascade Windows overlaps all open windows, revealing the title bar areas and resizing the windows equally

3 Show Windows Stacked resizes windows equally and displays them across the screen in rows

4 Show Windows Side by Side resizes windows equally and displays them across the screen in columns

...cont'd

When you have a number of windows open on the desktop, you might wish to see what's hidden underneath. For this, Windows 7 offers the Aero Peek function.

 Move the mouse pointer over the Show Desktop button, and open windows are replaced by outlines

This reveals the desktop icons and any Gadgets (see page 192) that you may have opened. To actually select any of these items:

 Click the Show desktop button, and all the open windows are minimized. Click again to redisplay the open windows

Note that you could instead right-click an empty part of the Taskbar, as shown on page 54, and select the option to Show the desktop (which then gets changed to Show open windows)

Hot tip

The Aero Peek feature is not available in the Starter or Home Basic editions of Windows 7.

Don't forget

The Show Desktop button is on the far right of the Taskbar, next to the notification area.

55

Hot tip

This Taskbar menu option is available in all the editions of Windows 7.

Aero Snaps

Aero Snaps provides a new set of methods for resizing and moving windows, mouse operated or using keyboard shortcuts.

Maximize Fully

Hot tip

Despite the name, the Aero Snaps feature is available in all editions of Windows 7.

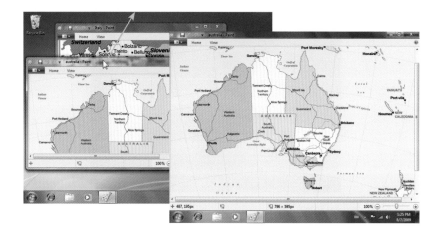

Left-click and hold the title bar area and drag the window up the screen. As the mouse pointer reaches the top edge of the screen, the window maximizes. The shortcut is WinKey+Up Arrow.

Maximize Vertically

Hot tip

If the window you want to maximize isn't the current window, click on it first, before carrying out the Maximize operation.

Don't forget

Alternatively, you can drag the bottom border of the window towards the bottom edge of the screen.

Click and hold the top border of the window and drag it towards the top edge of the screen. When the mouse pointer reaches the edge of the screen, the window will maximize in the vertical direction only. The shortcut is WinKey+Shift+Up Arrow.

Snap to the Left

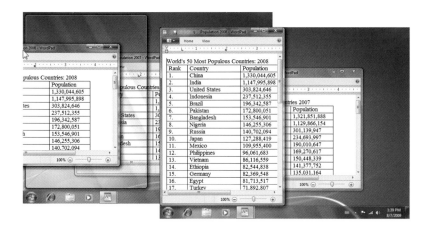

To position the window to fill the left hand side of the screen, click the Title bar and drag it to the left. As the mouse pointer reaches the left edge, the window resizes to fill half the screen. The shortcut is WinKey+Left Arrow.

Snap to the Right

To position the window to fill the right hand side of the screen, click the Title bar and drag it to the right. As the mouse pointer reaches the right edge, the window resizes to fill half the screen. The shortcut key is WinKey+Right Arrow.

Compare Two Windows

Snap one of the windows to the left and the other window to the right.

Restore

Drag the Title bar of a maximized or snapped window, away from the edge of the screen and the window will return to its previous size (though not the same position). The shortcut is WinKey+Down Arrow.

Hot tip

Alternatively, make the two windows the only open (not minimized) windows, right-click the Taskbar, and then choose the option to Show windows side-by-side. This works in all editions of Windows 7.

Hot tip

Double-clicking the Title bar will also reverse the maximize or snap. This restores size and position.

Switching Windows

If you have several windows open on your desktop, one will be active. This will be the foremost window and it has its Title bar, Menu bar and outside window frame highlighted. If you have more than one window displayed on the desktop, click anywhere inside a window that is not active to activate it and switch to it.

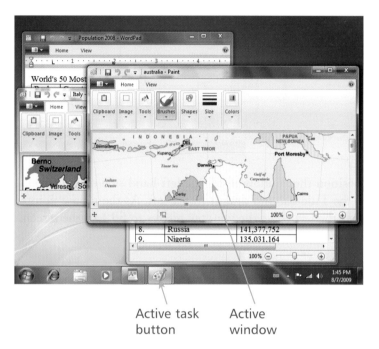

Active task button   Active window

Another method of switching windows is to use the Taskbar at the bottom. Every window that is open has a button created automatically on the Taskbar. Therefore, it does not matter if the window you want to switch to is overlaid with others and you cannot see it. Just click on the button for it in the Taskbar and the window will be moved to the front and made active.

Move the mouse pointer over a task button, and a live preview is displayed (one for each window if there are multiple for that task).

Windows Flip and Flip 3D

To use Windows Flip, hold down the Alt key and press Tab one or more times. This displays miniatures of all the windows and selects the next one in turn. Release Alt to make a window active.

Press WinKey+Tab to use the Flip 3D function to file through the open windows with large images in a perspective layout.

If you are running Windows 7 Starter edition, or if your computer is unable to support Aero features, there is no Live Preview for the tasks, though they are named and selectable from the Taskbar.

There is still an Alt+Tab Windows Flip feature, but it displays icons rather than previews of windows.

Don't forget

On the desktop, all windows except the one currently being selected are shown as outlines, as for Aero Peek (see page 55).

Hot tip

Pressing Alt+Tab once will act as a toggle, that switches you back and forth between the first two windows in the set.

Beware

Without Aero support, there is no WinKey+Alt Flip 3D feature available.

Arranging Icons

	Menu bar
✓	Details pane
	Preview pane
✓	Navigation pane

You can rearrange the order of the items in your folders or on your desktop in many different ways.

1 Right-click in a clear area (of the desktop or folder window) to display a shortcut menu

2 Move the pointer over Sort By, to reveal the submenu of sorting options and click e.g. the Name option, to sort all the file icons in ascending name order

3 Select Name a second time and the files will be sorted in descending name order

Group By

▓	Extra Large Icons
▤	Large Icons
▦	Medium Icons
▦	Small Icons
▤	List
▤	Details
▤	Tiles
▤	Content

You can select Group By for folder windows (but not for the Desktop). This groups your files and folders alphabetically by name, size, type etc. (see page 81 for more details). This option is used in the Computer folder, to display all your storage devices by type.

Scrolling

If a window is not big enough to display all the information within it, then a Scroll bar will appear automatically. Use it to see the contents of a window not immediately in view.

Scroll Up arrow

Scroll slider

Scroll bar

Scroll Down arrow

1 Drag the Scroll box along the Scroll bar towards one of the two Scroll arrows to scroll in that direction

2 Click the Scroll bar above or below the scroll slider to display the next window of information

3 Click one of the Scroll arrows to scroll just a little in that direction. Hold down the mouse button to keep scrolling

If your mouse has a wheel, you can use this to scroll. To set the increment:

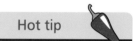 **Mouse**

1 Click Start, then type *Mouse* and press Enter

2 Select the Wheel tab to view and change the scroll settings

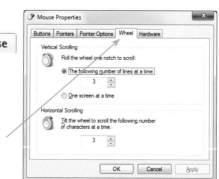

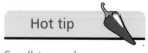
61

Closing a Window

When you've finished with a window you will need to close it. There are several ways of doing this – use the method that's easiest and the most appropriate at the time.

Open Window
If the top right corner of the window is visible on the desktop:

 Click the Close button on the Title bar

Minimized Window
For a window that's minimized or one that's hidden behind other windows:

 Move the mouse pointer over the associated task button

 Click the Close on the Live Preview for the task

Control Menu
If only part of the window is visible on the desktop:

 Click the Control icon (top left corner) or right-click the Title bar

 Click Close on the Control menu

Keyboard
To close any type of window use this key combination.

 Click the window to make it the current, active window, then press Alt+F4 to close the window

---

Don't forget

Save your work before closing any program window in which you've been working. However, Windows will prompt you if you forget.

Hot tip

Right-click the task button and select Close from the Jump List (see page 103). If there are multiple tasks of the same type, the option offered is Close all windows.

4 Windows Explorer

You'll find yourself using Windows Explorer to browse all the information on your computer and on the local network, whether you start from Computer or Documents or another Library, or open Windows Explorer explicitly as an application. In all cases, you can modify the view, sort the contents and customize the style and appearance.

64   Windows Explorer

65   Computer Folder

66   Exploring Drives

68   Opening Windows Explorer

69   Navigation Pane

70   Libraries

72   Customize the Library

74   Address Bar

76   Customize Layout

77   Folder Contents

78   Changing Views

79   Sorting

80   Filtering

81   Grouping

82   Folder Options

84   Customizing Folders

Windows Explorer

Windows Explorer is the first program used when you start up Windows 7. It manages the Start menu, desktop icons, file folders and special Start menu folders, and it appears on the Taskbar as a shortcut (with Internet Explorer and Windows Media Player).

To illustrate the range of functions that it supports:

1 Open programs (e.g. Notepad, and WordPad), folders (e.g. Computer, Documents, Music etc.) from the Start menu, and some customization and control functions

2 Windows of the same type will be grouped under a task button or a shortcut button if available

3 Move the mouse pointer over the Windows Explorer shortcut to see previews of the folder windows that Windows Explorer is managing

Since these tasks all use the same program, the techniques you learn when you open Computer, for example, will apply also in Documents or Pictures.

4 Move the mouse pointer over the other multiple Task button to see the customization and control windows

Hot tip

Windows Explorer (also known as Explorer) is the program Explorer.exe. It handles the file system and user interfaces, and is sometimes referred to as the Windows Shell.

Hot tip

When you right-click the desktop, you'll find customization functions, Screen Resolution and Personalize on the menu displayed.

Don't forget

To see what type of program any Task button represents, right-click it and display the Jump List (see page 103).

Computer Folder

The best way to look at the contents of your computer, involves using the Computer folder. To open this:

 1 Double-click the Computer icon on the desktop (if this icon is displayed)

2 Alternatively, click the Start button and select Computer from the Start menu

Don't forget

In previous versions of Windows, this folder was known as My Computer.

Navigation pane   Location   Search box

Hard disk drive

Removable devices CD/DVD or USB and also Floppy drives

Networked drive

Details pane

Don't forget

The Navigation pane provides the facilities you require to move between folders and drives.

65

 3 Select a drive and note how the contents of the Command bar change depending on the type of drive

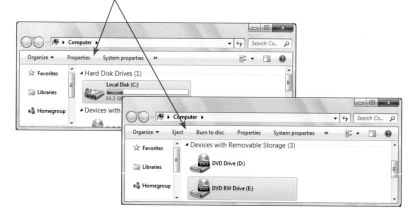

Hot tip

Windows Explorer adds the Eject button for a DVD or CD drive, plus the Burn to Disc button for rewriter capability.

Exploring Drives

Explore the contents of any drive from the Computer Folder.

Don't forget

As you explore a drive, the contents of the Command bar change to suit the particular entry selected.

1 Select one of the drive icons, for example, the USB removable storage device

Hot tip

Because the window has been resized, the Details pane gets hidden, This gives extra space for the contents. You can select this option for any size window (see page 76).

2 Double-click the USB device icon (or select it and press Enter) to display the files and folders that it contains

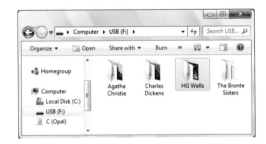

Don't forget

Press the Back arrow to return to the previous folder. See page 74 for more ways to navigate using the Address bar.

3 Double-click a folder entry (e.g. HG Wells) and select one of the files that it contains (e.g. The Invisible Man)

4 Double-click the file icon, or press Enter to open the file using the associated application e.g. Adobe Reader

...cont'd

You can see all the folder entries in Computer in a structured list.

1 Double-click the Computer entry in the Navigation pane

2 The Computer folder is displayed, and the fixed drives plus any removable drives with media inserted are listed

3 Click the ▷ open triangle next to a heading level, to expand that entry to the next level

4 Click the ◢ filled triangle to collapse the entries to that heading level

5 Right-click the Navigation pane and select Show all folders, to display your system in a folder list headed by the Desktop

6 Reselect Show all folders to revert to the separate groupings of folders

Don't forget

You can also explore the folders in your Favorites, Libraries, HomeGroup and Network of attached computers.

Hot tip

Resize the navigation pane horizontally using the stretch arrow, and traverse folder lists using the vertical scroll bar.

Hot tip

Click Expand to current folder, to expand the folder list to the currently selected folder.

67

Opening Windows Explorer

Viewing the Computer folder is just one way of opening Windows Explorer. There are a number of other ways.

 Select another folder from the Start menu, such as Documents, Pictures or Music to open it as a Library in Windows Explorer

2 Press the Windows Logo key + E combination, and Windows Explorer program opens with Computer folder

3 Right-click the Start button and select Start Windows Explorer. The current user's Libraries are shown

 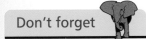
 Select Start, All Programs, Accessories and select the Windows Explorer entry, to start the program and display the Libraries folder

Navigation Pane

Whichever folder is initially displayed, the Navigation Pane allows you to select an alternative starting point. For example:

 Click the Favorites entry to display the list of shortcuts

 Click the open triangle or double-click the Favorites entry to expand the list of shortcuts

 Select one of the shortcuts, for example Downloads

 The related folder will be displayed and the folder list shown in the Navigation pane

To add a new shortcut to Favorites:

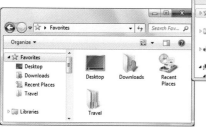

 Open the desired location, e.g. by exploring the drive or folder (see page 66)

Right-click Favorites and click Add current location to Favorites

 The shortcut is added to your Favorites

(see page 66)

Beware

The location must be actually open, not just selected in the current folder, otherwise the containing folder becomes the shortcut.

Libraries

Windows 7 introduces the Library, a new way of accessing the files on your computer and network. Each library displays files from several locations. Initially there are four libraries defined, showing files from the current user and the public folders:

Don't forget

These folders are stored by username, e.g. the music folder for the current user is at: C:\Users\Harshad\Music while the public (shared) music folder is at: C:\Users\Public\Music

- Documents –   My Documents, Public Documents
- Music –   My Music, Public Music
- Pictures –   My Pictures, Public Pictures
- Videos –   My Videos, Public Videos

To view the Pictures library for example:

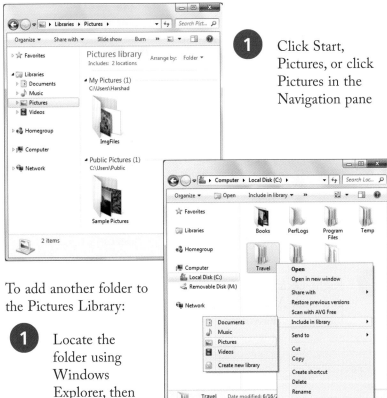

1 Click Start, Pictures, or click Pictures in the Navigation pane

Hot tip

You can also right-click the folder name in the Navigation pane folder list, to display the same menus.

To add another folder to the Pictures Library:

1 Locate the folder using Windows Explorer, then right-click the folder icon

2 Select Include in library, then select the required library, in this case Pictures, to add the folder

...cont'd

The selected folder and its subfolders are added to the library, and the contents of the whole collection are displayed in the default Folders arrangement. To select a different arrangement:

1 Click the arrow next to Arrange by and select for example Month

2 The files in the Pictures folders are re-organized by month of creation

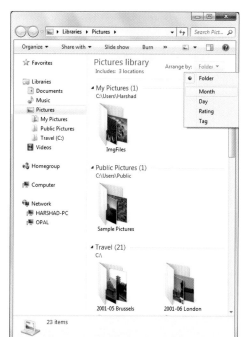

Hot tip

Note that there are now three locations in the Pictures library.

Don't forget

You can select a folder and choose to Create a new Library with it.

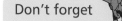

71

Don't forget

The icon for each group illustrates a selection of the pictures in that group, in a stack format.

3 The Details pane shows the number of groups, if no icon is selected. Click an individual icon, to see the number of pictures included in that portion of the collection

Customize the Library

You can view or change the way that a particular library operates:

 Open the library concerned, for example Pictures

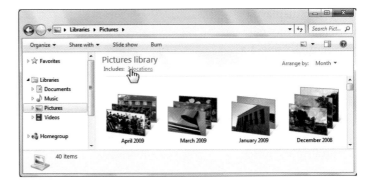

 Click Locations in the Library pane which lists the locations and shows the current default save location

 Select and right-click a library location and you can make it the default save location, or remove it, or reposition it

 Click the Add button to put more folders into the library

 Click the Remove button to remove the selected location. The button will be greyed (unavailable) if no location has been selected

72

...cont'd

The library can be optimized for a particular file type, for example pictures or music. This will change the options available for arranging the files and folders in the library. To view or change the type of file a library is optimized for:

 1 Open the Libraries folder and right-click the library and select Properties from the menu displayed

 2 Set the save location, or add a folder, or remove a folder from the library

 3 Show or hide the library on the Navigation pane

4 Click the bar Optimize this library for, to select a different file type

5 Click Restore Defaults to undo all changes

Hot tip

The initial four libraries are optimized for documents, music, pictures and videos respectively.

Hot tip

When you create a new library, the file type selected depends on the type of content. General Items will be selected for mixed file types.

73

Don't forget

If there's only one location in the library, the Set save location button is greyed and unavailable.

Address Bar

The Address bar at the top of Windows Explorer displays the current location as a set of names separated by arrows, and offers another way to navigate between libraries and locations.

Don't forget

Press the Back arrow to select the previous library or location, or click the down arrow to select from the list of viewed locations.

1 To go to a location that's named in the address, click on that name in the address bar, e.g. Documents

2 To select a subfolder of a library or location named in the Address bar, click the arrow to the right of that item

Hot tip

If the current location appears in the list, its name will be highlighted in bold print.

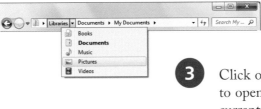

3 Click one of the entries to open it in place of the current location

When you are viewing a drive rather than a library, the address bar shows the drive and its folders, and allows you to navigate amongst these.

Don't forget

Press the Back arrow to select the previous folder or drive, or click the down arrow to select from the list of viewed folders.

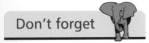

...cont'd

You can specify a new location using the address bar:

 Click the Address bar, in the space to the right of the set of names and the full path is displayed

 Type the complete folder path, e.g. *C:\Users\Public* (or click in the path and amend the values) then press Enter

 The specified location will be displayed

If you want a common location such as Desktop, just type the name alone and press Enter, and the location will be displayed:

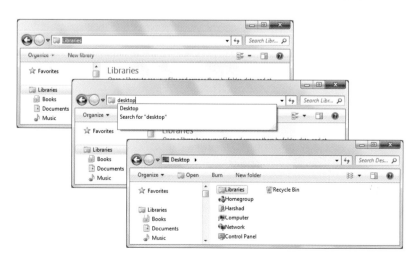

Hot tip

The path is highlighted, so typing a new path will completely replace the original values.

Don't forget

You can switch to exploring the Internet, by typing a web page address. Internet Explorer will be launched in a separate window.

Hot tip

The common locations include Computer, Contacts, Control Panel, Documents, Favorites, Games, Music, Pictures and Recycle Bin.

75

Customize Layout

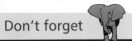

Don't forget

This menu also offers the Menu Bar option, to display the old-style Menu bar permanently. Pressing the Alt key also displays the Menu bar, but temporarily, just for one use.

Hot tip

The Preview button offers you a convenient way to show or hide the Preview pane.

Hot tip

The Games folder is an exception to the normal rule, since it does not feature the Navigation pane in its layout.

The normal view for Windows Explorer includes the Navigation pane and the Details pane, plus a Library pane where appropriate. There's also a Preview pane available.

You can choose which panes to display:

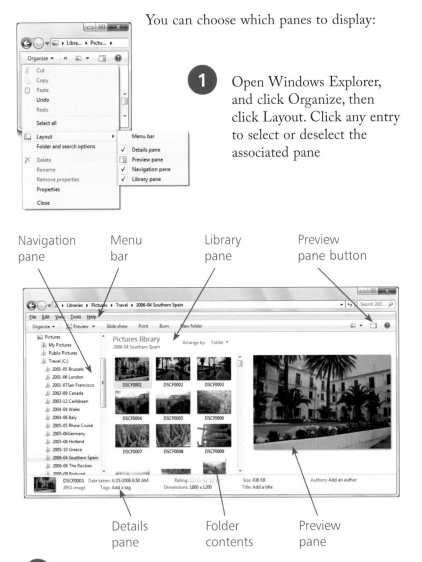

1 Open Windows Explorer, and click Organize, then click Layout. Click any entry to select or deselect the associated pane

Navigation pane   Menu bar   Library pane   Preview pane button

Details pane   Folder contents   Preview pane

2 Click any entry in the folder contents, to see an image of it in the Preview pane

3 Drag the separator lines between the panes, using the resize pointers (see page 50) to adjust the panes

Folder Contents

The entries in any of the folders you look at with Windows Explorer will be other folders and/or files (documents, pictures, programs etc.). The way these are presented will differ from folder to folder, based on the type of files normally contained:

Documents

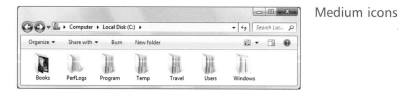

Details –

Name
Date modified
Type
Size

Music

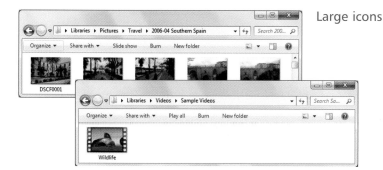

Details –

Name
Contributing artist
Album
Title etc

Pictures and Videos

Large icons

Subfolders

Medium icons

Hot tip

In these examples, the Navigation and Details panes have been turned off to concentrate on the folder contents.

Hot tip

Although both these folders use Details view, they show different sets of attributes appropriate to their types of file.

Don't forget

The display style for the contents in your own versions of these folders may be different but, whatever the settings, you can make changes to suit your preferences (see page 84).

Changing Views

You can change the size and appearance of the file and folder icons in your folders, using the Views menu on the Command bar.

 Open the folder you would like to change and click the arrow next to Views on the toolbar

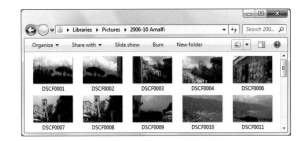

 Click and drag the slider to change the appearance of icons. Changes are applied as the slider moves

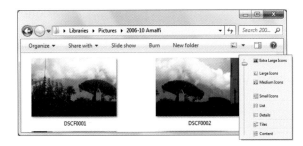

Hot tip

Click the Views button on the toolbar (not the down arrow), and you will switch to the next view in the sequence, cycling through List, Details, Tiles, Content and Large (skipping Extra Large, Medium and Small Icons).

Hot tip

You can move through intermediate positions, but as the slider approaches one of the four icon sizes, it snaps to that position. There are no intermediate positions with List, Details, Tiles or Content.

Don't forget

Click an entry on the list to switch immediately to that setting.

 Pause at any position, holding the mouse button, to see the effect. Release the mouse button to apply that view

This illustrates the new Content view, that has been added to Windows 7. The details depend on file type

Sorting

Windows 7 allows you to sort your files in the drive or folder by various attributes or descriptors.

 Open the folder, select Details view and click the attribute header that you want to sort by, e.g. Type

Hot tip

Windows Vista displays headers in any view. In Windows 7, only Details view displays headers, so you need to switch views to sort by header.

 The entries are sorted into ascending order by the selected attribute. The header is shaded and a sort symbol ∧ added

Hot tip

Note that any subfolders within your folder will be sorted to the end of the list, when you reverse the sequence. Libraries are an exception, and keep folders at the front (in the appropriate sort order).

 Click the header again, the order is reversed and the header now shows an inverted sort symbol ∨

4 The contents will remain sorted in the selected sequence, even if you switch to a different folder view

79

Filtering

Hot tip

This shows ranges of values appropriate to the particular attribute and based on the actual contents of the folder. These ranges are used for filtering and for grouping the items in the folder.

Hot tip

Filtering can only be applied in the Details folder view.

Hot tip

If you navigate away from the folder or close Windows Explorer, the next time you visit the folder, the filtering will have been removed.

 In the Details view, select any header and click the down arrow

 Click the box next to one or more ranges, and the items displayed are immediately restricted to that selection

3 You can select a second header, Size for example, to apply additional filtering to the items displayed

4 The tick ✓ symbol on headers indicates that filtering is in effect, and the address bar shows the attributes

 Filtering remains in effect even if you change folder views

Grouping

You can group the contents of the folder using the header ranges. You do not need to select the Details view.

Don't forget

The right-click menu also offers the Sort By option, so you can specify or change the sort sequence without switching to Details view.

1 Right-click an empty part of the folder area, move over (or click) Group By, then select an attribute e.g. Type

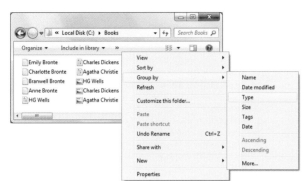

2 The contents will be grouped, using the ranges for the attribute selected

Hot tip

Any sorting that was already in place will remain in effect. However, you can switch between Ascending and Descending.

3 Grouping is retained when you switch views (and when you revisit the folder after closing Windows Explorer)

Expand Group

Collapse Group

(Folder Views other than List)

Hot tip

Select Group By, (None) to remove grouping. Select More... to add other attributes. The new attributes will also appear in Details view.

4 You can regroup the folder contents by selecting another attribute. This will replace your original choice

Folder Options

You can change the appearance and the behavior of your folders by adjusting the folder settings.

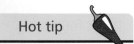
1 From any folder, click Organize and select Folder and Search Options

2 Choose Open each folder in its own window, to keep multiple folders open at the same time

3 If you want items to open as they do on a web page, select Single-click to open an item (point to select)

4 Control the way that the folder list expands on the Navigation pane

5 Click Apply to try out the selected changes without closing the Folder Options

6 Select Restore Defaults then Apply, to reset all options to their default values

There are further settings that can be applied to the current folder (from which the Folder Options were opened).

 From the Folder Options dialog box, click the View tab

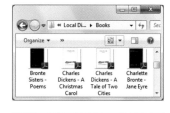

Folder Options

General | **View** | Search

Folder views

You can apply the view (such as Details or Icons) that you are using for this folder to all folders of this type.

[Apply to Folders]   [Reset Folders]

Advanced settings:

- Files and Folders
  - ☐ Always show icons, never thumbnails
  - ☐ Always show menus
  - ☑ Display file icon on thumbnails
  - ☑ Display file size information in folder tips
  - ☐ Display the full path in the title bar (Classic theme only)
  - Hidden files and folders
    - ◉ Don't show hidden files, folders, or drives
    - ○ Show hidden files, folders, and drives
  - ☑ Hide empty drives in the Computer folder
  - ☑ Hide extensions for known file types
  - ☑ Hide protected operating system files (Recommended)

[Restore Defaults]

[OK]   [Cancel]   [Apply]

(Hot tip, right column)

Hot tip

Click the Apply to Folders button to apply the current folder view to all folders of the same type. If you open Folder Options from the Control Panel, rather than a folder, this button becomes inactive.

Hot tip

This dialog box provides Always show menus, another place where you can switch on the classic menu bar for folders.

83

2 Clear the option Display file icon on thumbnails, then click Apply to remove the branding that indicates the file type on the file previews

3 Click Always show icons, never thumbnail previews, press Apply and you may find that you get better performance with the use of static file icons

Hot tip

To avoid having to create an individual miniature of each document or image, the standard icon for the file type is displayed.

4 Click Restore Defaults if you want to undo all the changes

Customizing Folders

1 Open the folder, right-click a clear space within it and select Customize this folder

Customize this folder...

2 Click the down arrow on the box under Optimize this folder for, then choose the most relevant type e.g. General Items

3 Click Choose File, locate an image file and click Open and Apply to the folder

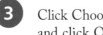

Restore Default

5 Manage Files and Folders

Folders can contain other folders as well as files, and Windows treats them in very much the same way. Hence operations such as moving, copying , deleting and searching apply to files and to folders in a similar way, while compressed files (which contain files and folders) are treated as folders in their own right.

86 Select Files and Folders

88 Copy or Move Files or Folders

92 File Conflicts

94 Delete Files and Folders

95 The Recycle Bin

98 Create a File or Folder

99 Rename a File or Folder

100 Backtrack File Operations

101 File Properties

102 Open Files

103 Recent Items

104 Search for Files and Folders

105 Compressed Folders

107 Fonts Folder

108 Character Map

Select Files and Folders

Single File or Folder

1 Left-click the item to highlight it, then move, copy or delete it as required

Sequential Files

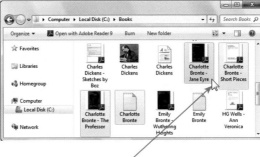

1 Click to select the first item, press and hold Shift, then click the last item in the range, to highlight the range

Adjacent Block

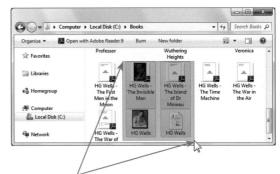

1 Drag out a box to cover the files you want selected. All the files in that rectangular area will be highlighted

Non-adjacent Files

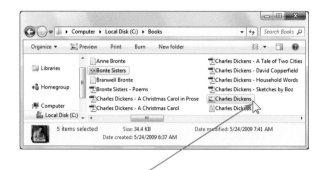

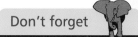
1 To select several non-adjacent files, click one item, press and hold Ctrl, then click the subsequent items. As you select files, they are highlighted

Partial Sequence

You can combine these techniques to select part of a range.

1 Select a group of sequential files or an adjacent block of files (as described on page 86)

2 Hold down Ctrl, and click to deselect any files in the range that you do not want and to select any extra ones

All Files and Folders

To select all the files (and folders) in the current folder, click Organize and choose Select All or press Ctrl+A.

Copy or Move Files or Folders

You may wish to copy or move some files and folders, to another folder on the same drive, or to another drive. There are several ways to achieve this.

Drag, Using the Right Mouse Button

 Open Windows Explorer and the folder with the required files, then locate the destination in the Folders list

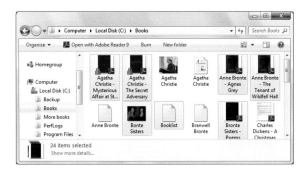

In the folder contents, select the files and folders that you want to copy or move

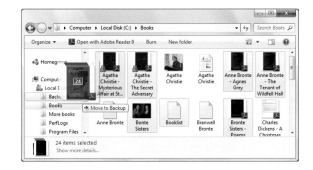

Right-click any one of the selection, drag the files onto the destination folder or drive in the Folders list, so it is highlighted and named, then release to display the menu

Click the Move Here or Copy Here option as desired, and the files will be added to the destination folder

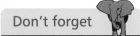

Drag, Using the Left Mouse Button

In this case default actions are applied, with no intervening menu.

1 Select the files and folders to be moved or copied

2 Use the left mouse button to drag the selection to the destination drive or folder in the Folders list, in this example the removable USB storage drive

3 Press Shift to Move instead of Copy to another drive. Press Ctrl to Copy instead of Move to a folder on the same drive as the source folder

In Summary

Drives	Drag	Drag+Shift	Drag+Ctrl
Same	Move	Move	Copy
Different	Copy	Move	Copy

...cont'd

Using Cut, Copy, Paste

Cut doesn't remove the selection initially, it just dims it, until you Paste it (see step 5). Press Esc if you decide to cancel the move, and the item will remain in place.

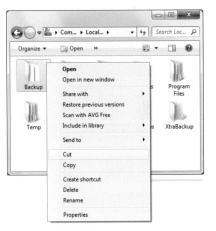

1 Choose the files and folders you want to copy and right-click within the selection

2 From the shortcut menu click Copy or click Cut to move the selection

3 Right-click and click Open in new windows, for the folder in which you want to put the selection

Select Send To, to direct the selected files and folders to a device with removable storage, e.g. a USB drive.

4 Right-click a blank area of the destination folder

5 Click Paste from the menu to complete the copy or move operation

When you Copy, you can Paste Shortcut (instead of Paste) to insert a link to the original file. However, this is inactive when you Cut files.

Keyboard Shortcuts

Cut, Copy and Paste options are also available as keyboard shortcuts. Select files and folders as above, but use these keys in place of the menu selections for Copy, Cut and Paste. There are also shortcuts to Undo an action or Redo an action.

Press this key	To do this
F1	Display Help
Ctrl+C	Copy the selected item
Ctrl+X	Cut the selected item
Ctrl+V	Paste the selected item
Ctrl+Z	Undo an action
Ctrl+Y	Redo an action

Burn to Disc

If your computer has a CD or DVD recorder, you can copy files to a writable disc. This is usually termed burning.

1 Insert a writable CD or DVD disc into the recorder drive (DVD/CD RW)

2 When the Autoplay prompt appears, choose the option to Burn files to disc using Windows Explorer

3 Amend the suggested disc title if desired

4 Choose how you plan to use the disc you will be creating

5 By default, Windows uses the Live File System (UDF) format, but for compatibility with other devices, choose the Mastered (ISO) format

6 You can now copy or move files to the drive folder. When you have finished adding files, click Burn to disc

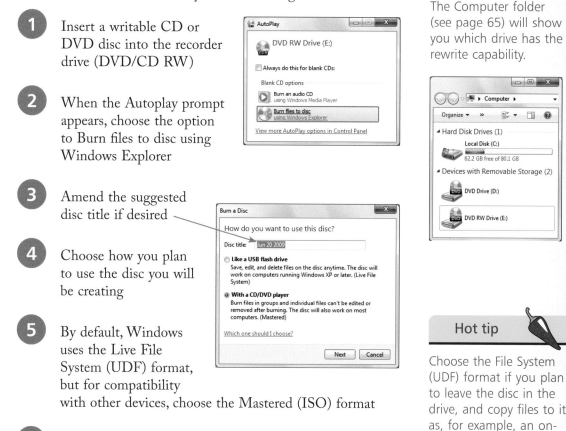

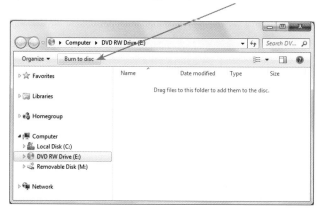

Don't forget

The Computer folder (see page 65) will show you which drive has the rewrite capability.

91

Hot tip

Choose the File System (UDF) format if you plan to leave the disc in the drive, and copy files to it as, for example, an on-going backup.

Don't forget

You can use any of the methods described for copying or moving one, or more, files and folders (see page 88).

File Conflicts

When you copy or move files from one folder to another, conflicts may arise. There may already be a file with the same name in the destination folder. To illustrate what may happen:

 Open the More books folder and the Backup folder

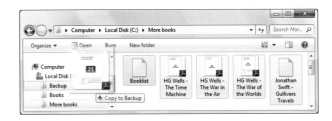

Don't forget

Hold down the Ctrl key as you drag, if the Backup folder is on the same drive as the More books folder.

 Press Ctrl+A in Documents, and Drag the selection onto the Backups folder, to initiate a copy of all the files

Hot tip

If you know that your source folder contains the most up-to-date version of all the files, you should select Copy and Replace, then click the box to Do this for all the remaining conflicts (in this case, 4 more).

 Windows observes a conflict – this file already exists, with identical size and date information. Select Don't Copy

4 The next case is where the source file is newer and larger than the existing file. Assuming that this is an updated version, click Copy and Replace

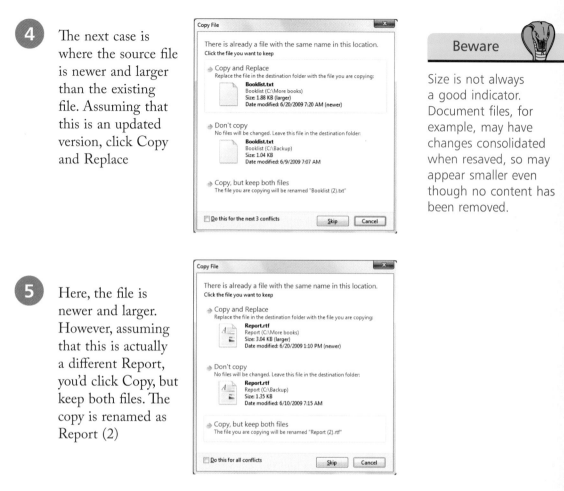

5 Here, the file is newer and larger. However, assuming that this is actually a different Report, you'd click Copy, but keep both files. The copy is renamed as Report (2)

6 The Backup folder now has updated copies of all the files, plus two different Report files

Delete Files and Folders

Don't forget

When you delete files and folders from your hard disk drive, they are actually moved to a temporary storage area, the Recycle Bin, described on the following page.

When you want to remove files or folders, you use the same delete procedures – whatever drive or device the items are stored on.

1 Choose one or more files and folders, selected as described previously (see page 86)

2 Right-click the selection and click Delete

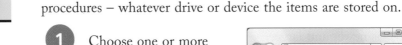

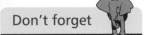

Hot tip

You can press the Delete key on your keyboard, after selecting the files and folders, instead of using the menus.

3 Alternatively, having selected the items, click Organize and then select Delete

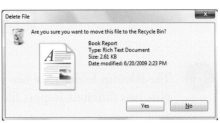

Don't forget

You may need to have administrator authority to delete some files or folders.

4 You get an Are You Sure message, whether there are multiple files or a single file involved. Click Yes to confirm, or No to cancel deletion

If you choose to delete then immediately realize that you have made a mistake deleting one or more files, right-click the folder area and select Undo Delete or press Ctrl+Z, to reverse the last operation. For hard disk items, you are also able to retrieve deleted files from the Recycle Bin, and this could be a substantial time later.

The Recycle Bin

The Recycle Bin is, in effect, a folder on your hard disk drive that holds deleted files and folders. They are not physically removed from your hard disk (unless you empty the Recycle Bin or delete specific items from within the Recycle Bin itself). They will remain there, until the Recycle Bin fills up, at which time the oldest deleted files may be finally removed.

The Recycle Bin, therefore, provides a safety net for files and folders you may delete by mistake and allows you to easily retrieve them, even at a later date.

Restoring Files

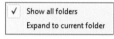

1 Double-click on the Recycle Bin icon from the desktop or in the Computer folder

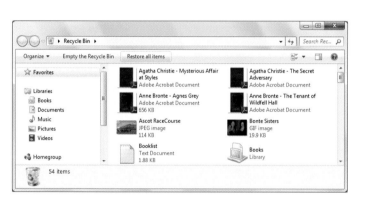

2 Click the Restore all items button, or select a file and the button changes to Restore this item

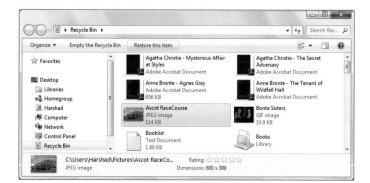

95

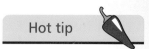
Don't forget

To see where the Recycle Bin is located, right-click the Navigation pane and select Show all folders.

Don't forget

If you select multiple files or folders the button will become Restore the selected items.

Hot tip

A restored folder will include all the files and subfolders that it held when it was originally deleted.

...cont'd

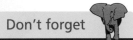
Permanently Erase Files
You may want to explicitly delete particular files, perhaps for reasons of privacy and confidentiality.

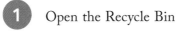 Open the Recycle Bin

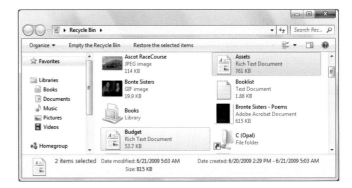

 Select the relevant files and folders, then select Delete from the one of the menus (or press the Delete key)

 Click Yes, to confirm that you want to permanently delete these files (completely remove from the hard disk drive)

Empty the Recycle Bin
If desired, you can remove all of the contents of the Recycle Bin from the hard disk drive.

 With the Recycle Bin open, click the Empty the Recycle Bin button

 Press Yes to confirm the permanent deletion

The Recycle Bin icon changes from full to empty, to illustrate the change.

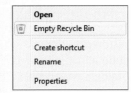

Bypass the Recycle Bin

If you want to prevent particular deleted files from being stored in the Recycle Bin:

  Select the files and folders, right-click the selection (as described on page 94) but this time, hold down the Shift key as you select Delete

 Confirm that you want to permanently delete the selected item or items. "Permanent" means that no copy will be kept

(as described on page 94)

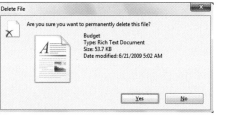

Deactivate (or Resize) the Recycle Bin

You can tell Windows to always bypass the Recycle Bin.

Right-click the Recycle Bin icon, then select Properties from the menu

Note the space available on Recycle Bin location (free space on hard disk)

Adjust the maximum size allowed, to resize the Recycle Bin

Click the button labelled "Don't move files to the Recycle Bin. Remove files immediately when deleted." to always bypass Recycle Bin

---

Hot tip

You could also hold down the Shift key and select Delete from the Organize menu, or just press the Delete key on the keyboard.

Beware

Take extra care when selecting files and folders, if you are bypassing the Recycle Bin, since you'll have no recovery options.

Don't forget

This dialog box also allows you to suppress the warning message issued when you delete items.

Create a File or Folder

You can create a new folder in a drive, folder or on the desktop.

1 Right-click an empty part of the folder window and select New and then New Folder

2 Overtype the default name New Folder, e.g. type *Articles*, and press Enter

To create a new file in a standard format for use with one of the programs installed on your computer.

1 Right-click an empty part of the folder, select New, and choose the specific file type e.g. Rich Text File document

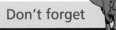

2 Overtype the file name provided and press Enter

Rename a File or Folder

You can rename a file or folder at any time, by simply editing the current name.

 Right-click the file/folder, then click Rename, or select the icon and click on the icon name

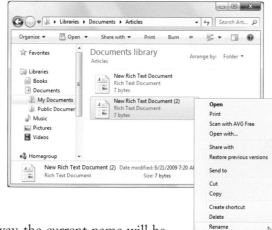

 Either way, the current name will be highlighted. Type a name to delete and replace the current name:

or press the arrow keys to position the typing cursor and edit the existing name:

Press Enter or click elsewhere to confirm the new name

Preserving File Types

When you have file extensions revealed (see page 98) and you create or rename a file or folder, only the name itself, not the file type, will be highlighted. This avoids accidental changes of type.

Use the same method to rename icons on the desktop. You can even rename the Recycle Bin.

You must always provide a non-blank file name, and you should avoid special characters such as quote marks, question marks and periods.

Beware

You can change the file type, but you will be warned that this may make the file unusable.

Backtrack File Operations

If you accidentally delete, rename, copy or move the wrong file or folder, you can undo (reverse) the last operation and preceding operations, to get back to where you started. For example:

1 Right-click the folder area and select the Undo Rename command that is displayed

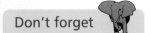

2 Right-click again, and this time there's an Undo Delete command for you to select

3 Now you will have reversed the last two operations, putting the folder and files back as they were before the changes

File Properties

Every file (and every folder) has information that can be displayed in the Properties dialog box. To display this:

1 Right-click the file or folder icon to display the shortcut menu

2 Click the Properties entry, to display details for the file

3 Right-click the folder icon and select Properties, to display the folder information

4 You can similarly display Properties for any of the Libraries (see page 70)

Hot tip

The purpose of the Properties dialog box is:
• to display details
• to change settings for the selected file or folder.

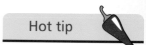

Hot tip

You may find additional entries on your menu, inserted when you install a new application program (see page 119).

Don't forget

Click Security and other tabs, to display more information about the file or folder, and click the Advanced button for additional attributes.

Open Files

You can open a file, using an associated program but without having first to explicitly start that program. There are several ways to do this:

Default Program

 Double-click the file icon

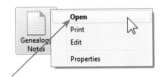

 Right-click the file and click Open from the menu

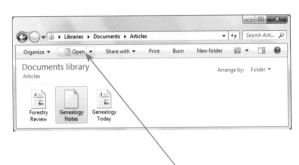

 Select the file, then click Open on the Command bar

Alternative Program

You may have several programs that can open a particular file type. To use a different program than the default to open the file:

 Right-click the file icon and select Open with. Pick a program from the list or click Choose default program to set a new default program

 The same choices are presented, when you click the down arrow next to the Open button on the Command bar in the folder window

Recent Items

Quite often you'll want to open a document you have been working on recently. Windows stores details of the latest documents you've been using. To see the list of recent documents:

 1 Click Start, and move the mouse pointer over the entry for the application, for example WordPad

2 The Jump list expands, showing recent items

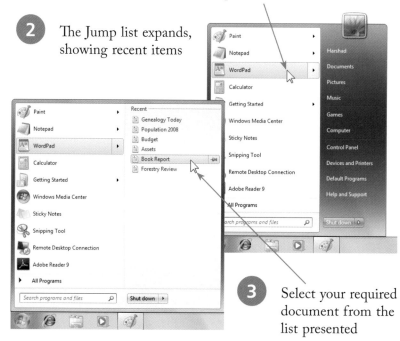

3 Select your required document from the list presented

Clear Recent Items

You can clear the history that appears in the Recent Items.

1 Right-click the Start button and select Properties

2 Clear the box Store and display recently opened items in the Start menu and the taskbar

3 Click the Apply button and the list will be cleared. Reselect the box to resume recording

Don't forget

Like Vista, Windows 7 has a Recent Items entry for the Start menu, with documents from multiple applications, but this is superseded by Jump Lists and is normally disabled.

Don't forget

If the application is currently active, right-click its button on the taskbar to see the list of recent items.

Search for Files and Folders

If you are not quite sure where exactly you stored a file, or what the full name is, the folder Search box may be the answer.

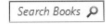
1 Open a location e.g. Documents, click in the Search box and start typing a word from the file e.g. *charles*

2 If that produces too many files, start typing another word that might help limit the number of matches e.g. *darwin*

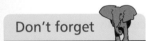
3 If the location is a drive rather than a library, its contents may not be indexed, so the search may take longer

Compressed Folders

This feature allows you to save disk space by compressing files and folders while allowing them to be treated as normal by Windows.

Create a Compressed Folder

 Right-click an empty portion of the folder window and select New, Compressed (zipped) Folder

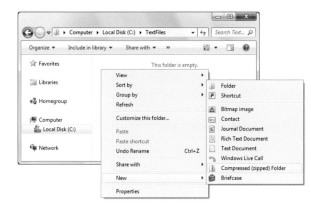

 A compressed folder is created, with default name New Compressed (zipped) Folder.zip

 Rename it (see page 99). You can also open, move, or delete it just like any folder

Add Files or Folders to a Compressed Folder

 Drag files or folders onto a compressed folder and they will automatically be compressed and stored there

Hot tip

Compressed folders are distinguished from other folders by a zipper on the folder icon. They are compatible with other zip archive programs, such as Winzip.

Don't forget

To create a compressed folder and copy a file into it at the same time: right-click a file, select Send To, Compressed (zipped) Folder. The new compressed folder has the same file name, but a file extension of .zip.

Hot tip

The compressed folder is treated like a separate device. By default, files will be copied rather than moved when they are dragged to, or from, the folder.

...cont'd

Compressed Item Properties

1 Double-click the compressed folder and select any file to see the compressed size versus the actual size

Don't forget

Right-click the file and select Properties to display this information, if the Details panel has not been enabled.

Extract Files and Folders

1 Open the compressed folder, drag files and folders onto a normal folder and they'll be decompressed. The compressed version still remains in the compressed folder, unless you hold the Shift key as you drag (i.e. Move)

Extract All

1 To extract all of the files and folders from a compressed folder, right-click it and then click on Extract All

| Open |
| Open in new window |
| Extract All... |
| Scan with AVG Free |
| Open with... |
| Restore previous versions |
| Send to |
| Cut |
| Copy |
| Create shortcut |
| Delete |
| Rename |
| Properties |

2 Accept or edit the target folder and click Extract. The files and folders are decompressed and transferred

Hot tip

If the folder specified does not exist, it will be created automatically.

Extract Compressed (Zipped) Folders

Select a Destination and Extract Files

Files will be extracted to this folder:

C:\TextFiles\Classics   Browse...

☑ Show extracted files when complete

Extract   Cancel

Fonts Folder

Windows includes several hundred different fonts. These offer a wide range of distinctive and artistic effects in windows and documents, and support multiple languages and special symbols.

To view the fonts available on your system:

 1 Select Start, Control Panel and Fonts from Appearance and Personalization (or click Fonts in View by Icons)

2 The Fonts folder is displayed in Windows Explorer

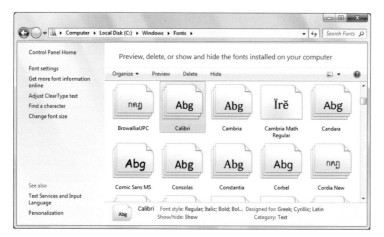

3 Double-click a group font such as Calibri to see the font styles that it contains

Don't forget

You can also find the Fonts folder within the C:\Windows folder.

Hot tip

Double-click a font to see samples of the characters at various point sizes.

107

Hot tip

Most of the Windows fonts will be TrueType or OpenType fonts which can be scaled to any size and can be sent to any printer or other output device that is supported by Windows.

Character Map

As well as letters and numbers, the fonts contain many special characters, not all of which appear on your computer keyboard. You can insert these characters into your documents using the Character Map, or by pressing particular key combinations.

1 In the Fonts folder select Find a character to display the Character Map application

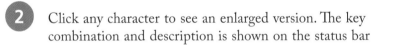

2 Click any character to see an enlarged version. The key combination and description is shown on the status bar

3 Click Select to add the character to the copy box, and click Copy to transfer selected characters to the clipboard

4 Click the Font box to select a different font from the list, for example Wingdings

6 Working with Programs

Windows provides the operational environment in which you can run application programs. It offers Start menu and search facilities to help you locate and run the applications, and helps you to install, organize and manage your programs effectively. It includes functions such as the Compatibility Wizard, XP Mode and Task Manager.

110 Start and Close Programs

112 Start Menu Searches

113 Create a Shortcut

114 Pin to Start Menu

115 Pin to Taskbar

116 Taskbar Grouping

117 Startup Folder

118 Minimized (or Maximized)

119 Install and Uninstall

120 Windows Features

121 Program Compatibility

122 Windows Virtual PC

124 Configure XP Mode

126 Command Prompt

128 Task Manager

130 Resource Monitor

Start and Close Programs

The Windows Start button enables you to quickly start any program installed in your computer.

1 Click on the Start button and the Start menu appears, with the most recently used programs and the Folders list

The most recently used (MRU) programs list will show recently installed applications, which appear for a short time at the bottom of the list. You can also pin your choice of entries above the MRU list on the Start menu (see page 114).

Hot tip

When you install new programs, their entries automatically appear in the All Programs list, positioned alphabetically, or in a new folder within All Programs.

Beware

Windows 7 does not support the Classic Start menu as used in previous versions of Windows.

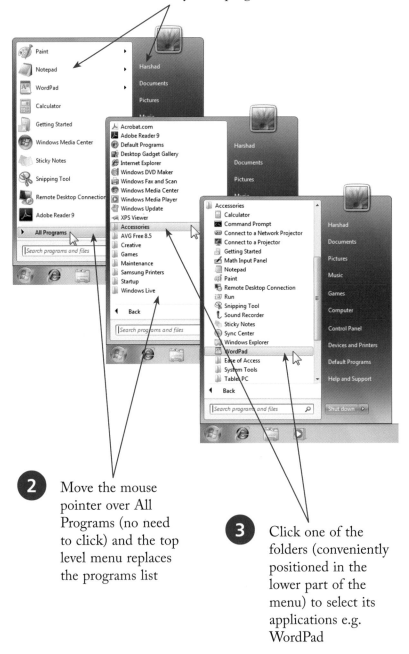

2 Move the mouse pointer over All Programs (no need to click) and the top level menu replaces the programs list

3 Click one of the folders (conveniently positioned in the lower part of the menu) to select its applications e.g. WordPad

4 When you select the WordPad application, it will open in a new window

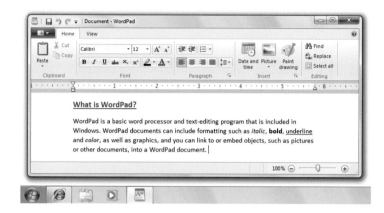

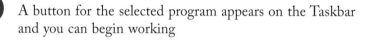

Don't forget

The WordPad application may also appear on the top level Start menu, if it has been used recently.

5 A button for the selected program appears on the Taskbar and you can begin working

Close the Program
There are several ways to close the program.

1 Click the Close button on the top right of the window

Don't forget

These are analogous to the methods for closing a window (see page 62).

2 Select File, Exit from the Menu

3 Press Alt+F4

4 Click the Control icon, right-click the title bar or right-click the task button and select Close

Hot tip

You can also close the application and its window from the button on the taskbar. Right-click and select Close.

Restore	
Move	
Size	
Minimize	
Maximize	
Close	Alt+F4

If any changes have been made to the document, you may receive a warning message advising you to Save the associated file.

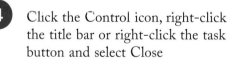

WordPad

Do you want to save changes to Document?

Save | Don't Save | Cancel

Recent
Budget 2010
Assets

WordPad
Pin this program to taskbar
Close window

Start Menu Searches

The Start menu gives you a very easy way to locate programs (and data files), if you are not sure where they are stored.

1 Click the Start button to open the Start menu

Don't forget

Case does not matter, but it is important to get the spelling right.

2 Start typing a word that is associated with the program you want, for example *View* (no need to click the box)

Hot tip

Search looks at the program titles in the Start menu, at file names and contents in the current user name, and in standard folders such as Program Files. You can extend the search scope by specifying the drive letter for an attached device.

Don't forget

You can also start a program by pressing the Windows Logo key + R to display the Run command, then enter the program name.

3 As you type, relevant programs and data files are displayed. When the one you are seeking appears, click it to start the program, or for a data file to open it using the associated program for that file type

Create a Shortcut

A Shortcut can save the location and provide easy access to a program you use frequently. To place the shortcut on the desktop:

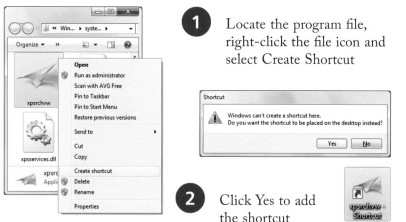

1 Locate the program file, right-click the file icon and select Create Shortcut

2 Click Yes to add the shortcut

Shortcuts can also be created to access other objects, including documents, folders, disk drives, printers and network devices.

1 Locate the item and drag its icon onto the desktop (or onto a folder) using the right mouse button

2 Drop the icon to display the menu,

3 Click Create Shortcuts Here to add the icon

4 Double-click the shortcut icon to open the drive (or start the associated application)

Beware

Windows will not let you create shortcuts in system folders or in special folders such as Computer, Network or Control Panel.

Don't forget

The shortcut copies the original icon, with the addition of a small arrow and the term – Shortcut.

Hot tip

If you delete a shortcut, the file that it relates to is not automatically deleted. The converse is also true – deleting the original item does not remove the shortcut.

113

Pin to Start Menu

Another way to get easy access to a program that you use often, is to add it to the top level on the Start menu

 Right-click the program icon or a shortcut to the program

 Select Pin to Start Menu

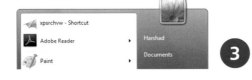

 The program is added above the MRU entries

Any existing most recently used entry for the program will be removed, when the program is pinned to the Start menu.

Folder Entries

To add a folder or folder shortcut to the Start menu

 Drag the icon over the Start button. When the Start menu expands, drop the icon at the top – the black line shows the position

Unpin Entries

To remove an entry that has been pinned to the Start menu:

 For programs, right-click the entry and select Unpin from Start Menu

For folders, right-click the entry and select Remove from this list

Where appropriate, programs may reappear in the MRU list.

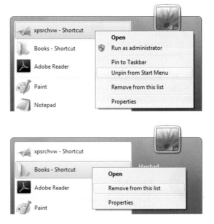

Pin to Taskbar

Windows 7 adds the facility to pin programs to the taskbar, and by default has three programs predefined: Internet Explorer, Windows Explorer and Windows Media Player. To add others:

1 Right-click the program icon or shortcut, and select Pin to Taskbar

2 A button for that program will appear on the taskbar

Don't forget

An MRU entry for that program on the Start menu will be removed (but an entry pinned to the Start menu will remain).

3 Right-click the taskbar entry to display recent items for that program, or to select Unpin this program from taskbar

If you have an application open, you can pin it to the taskbar:

1 Right-click the task button and select Pin this program to taskbar

Hot tip

When you right-click one of the task buttons or launch buttons, you can view and remove entries on the Recent list.

Folders on the Taskbar

You can also pin folders to the Taskbar via the Windows Explorer launch button:

1 Drag folder or its shortcut onto the taskbar and release it, to pin it to Windows Explorer

2 Right-click the Windows Explorer button to view the recent locations and pinned locations

Taskbar Grouping

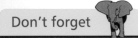
Windows creates a task button on the Taskbar for every document you open with a program. This can result in a very cluttered Taskbar, making it difficult to locate a particular task when you need to switch to it.

To reduce the confusion, Windows 7 uses taskbar grouping and combines all the tasks for the same program into just one task button. On the example taskbar there's 1 Internet Explorer task, 2 Windows Explorer tasks, 2 WordPad, 1 Notepad and 2 Paint.

Aero Peek Preview helps you identify which task is active in which window

 Move the mouse over a task button

However, you can ask Windows to display an individual button on the taskbar for each task.

1 Right-click the Start button and select Properties

2 Click the Taskbar tab

3 Click the Taskbar buttons box and select Combine when taskbar is full (or Never Combine)

You'll now see individual task buttons for each open window, with part of each document title (filename) displayed.

Startup Folder

The Startup feature allows a program or several programs to start automatically when you log on to Windows. Therefore, you can start work straightaway on a program that you always use.

 1 Create shortcuts on the desktop (see page 113) for the programs or documents you want to startup automatically

 2 Select Start, All Programs then right-click the Startup folder and select Open

3 Drag the shortcuts from the desktop into the Startup folder (see page 88 for moving items to a folder)

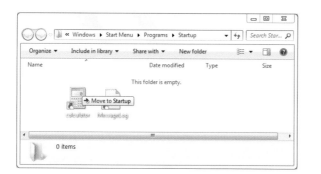

4 The shortcuts will now appear in the Startup folder in the All Programs part of the Start menu

Whenever Windows starts up from this point on, the Calculator program will be launched, and Notepad (the program associated with text files) will start up with the MessageLog text file displayed.

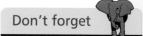

Don't forget

If you drag a shortcut to a document file into the Startup folder, the associated program will start up with that document displayed, whenever you start up Windows.

Hot tip

When you install new applications, these may also add programs to the Startup folder.

Minimized (or Maximized)

Sometimes you may want to start a program but not use it right away. You therefore need to set it up so that when it's started it is minimized automatically. When you are ready to use the program, you only need to click on its task button on the Taskbar.

1 Create a shortcut for a program you want to start minimized (see page 113)

Open
Open file location
Print
Edit
Scan with AVG Free
Open with
Restore previous versions
Send to
Cut
Copy
Create shortcut
Delete
Rename
Properties

2 Right-click on the shortcut program icon and then select Properties from the menu

3 Click the Shortcut tab

MessageLog Properties

General | Shortcut | Security | Details | Previous Versions

MessageLog

Target type: Text Document

Target location: Documents

Target: C:\Users\Harshad\Documents\MessageLog.txt

Start in: C:\Users\Harshad\Documents

Shortcut key: None

Run: Normal window

Comment:

Open File Location | Change Icon... | Advanced...

OK | Cancel | Apply

4 Click the down arrow for Run and select Minimized

Normal window
Minimized
Maximized

...rties

...ecurity | Details | Previous Versions

...eLog

Target type: Text Document

Target location: Documents

Target: C:\Users\Harshad\Documents\MessageLog.txt

Start in: C:\Users\Harshad\Documents

Shortcut key: None

Run: Minimized

Comment: Starts up in Notepad, minimized

Open File Location | Change Icon... | Advanced...

OK | Cancel | Apply

5 Add a comment if you wish, then click OK to save the change

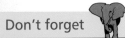

Install and Uninstall

If the program you want to install is provided on CD or DVD, you normally just insert the disc. The installation program starts up automatically and you can follow the instructions to select features and complete the installation.

If the installation does not start automatically, you can use the Run command to start the program manually (see page 112), or examine the contents of the disc using Windows Explorer.

To review your existing installed programs:

1 Select Start, Control Panel then select Uninstall a Program, in the Programs section

2 Select a program and you'll be offered options such as Uninstall, Change or Repair

3 Click View Installed Updates for the record of changes that have been applied to your system

Hot tip

The installation program is often called Setup.exe or Install.exe, though this does vary from product to product.

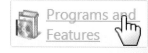

Don't forget

If you choose to view the Control Panel by Icons, you would double-click Programs and Features.

Beware

Some programs require you to insert the original program CD before you can continue, so make sure that the CDs are available.

119

Windows Features

There are numerous components in Windows, some of which are made available at installation time, while others are turned off. In earlier versions of Windows you were required to uninstall or reinstall Windows components. However, in this version, the features remain installed at all times, you just specify whether they should be active or not.

1 Open the Uninstall a Program option (see page 119) and click the option Turn Windows features on or off

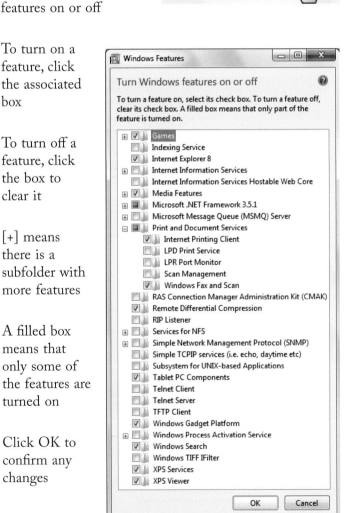

View installed updates

🛡 Turn Windows features on or off

2 To turn on a feature, click the associated box

3 To turn off a feature, click the box to clear it

4 [+] means there is a subfolder with more features

5 A filled box means that only some of the features are turned on

6 Click OK to confirm any changes

Windows Features

Turn Windows features on or off

To turn a feature on, select its check box. To turn a feature off, clear its check box. A filled box means that only part of the feature is turned on.

- ☑ Games
- ☐ Indexing Service
- ☑ Internet Explorer 8
- ☐ Internet Information Services
- ☐ Internet Information Services Hostable Web Core
- ☑ Media Features
- ■ Microsoft .NET Framework 3.5.1
- ☐ Microsoft Message Queue (MSMQ) Server
- ■ Print and Document Services
  - ☑ Internet Printing Client
  - ☐ LPD Print Service
  - ☐ LPR Port Monitor
  - ☐ Scan Management
  - ☑ Windows Fax and Scan
- ☐ RAS Connection Manager Administration Kit (CMAK)
- ☑ Remote Differential Compression
- ☐ RIP Listener
- ☐ Services for NFS
- ☐ Simple Network Management Protocol (SNMP)
- ☐ Simple TCPIP services (i.e. echo, daytime etc)
- ☐ Subsystem for UNIX-based Applications
- ☑ Tablet PC Components
- ☐ Telnet Client
- ☐ Telnet Server
- ☐ TFTP Client
- ☑ Windows Gadget Platform
- ☐ Windows Process Activation Service
- ☑ Windows Search
- ☐ Windows TIFF IFilter
- ☑ XPS Services
- ☑ XPS Viewer

OK   Cancel

Program Compatibility

If you have an older program or a game that was written specifically for a previous version of Windows, it might run poorly or not at all under Windows 7. If this is the case then:

 1 Open the Action Center and select Windows Program Compatibility Troubleshooter

 2 This will identify all the applications that may have problems. Select the one you want to work with

3 Allow Windows to apply the recommended settings, then try out the program to see if the problems are fixed

 4 If you find that the program now works, you can save the settings for use in future, otherwise try different settings

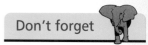
Don't forget

You'll find the Action Center in Control Panel, System and Security.

Action Center
Review your computer's status and resolve issues
Change User Account Control settings
Troubleshoot common computer problems
Restore your computer to an earlier time

Beware

Do not run Windows Program Compatibility troubleshooter on older antivirus programs or system programs, since these might cause data loss or create security issues.

Hot tip

Right-click the program icon, select Properties and the Compatibility tab to see the settings that have been applied.

Windows Virtual PC

Windows Virtual PC allows you to run your computer under Windows 7 operating system while maintaining compatibility with applications that run on older versions of Windows including Windows XP and Windows Vista.

If you are running Windows 7 Professional, Enterprise or Ultimate edition, there's extra support for Windows XP applications. You can use Windows XP mode to access a virtualized instance of Windows XP that is ready for you to customize with your own applications, without the need for a separate licensed copy of Windows XP.

Requirements

Windows Virtual PC requires hardware-assisted virtualization, available in processors with Intel Virtualization Technology (Intel VT) or AMD Virtualization (AMD-V) technology. You'll need to confirm that your computer includes this support and that it is enabled in the system BIOS. You also need at least a 1 GHz processor, 1.25 GB memory (2 GB recommended) and 15 GB hard disk space per virtual Windows environment.

To download the required installation files, go to the Windows Virtual PC website www.microsoft.com/windows/virtual-pc/

 1 Click Get Windows XP Mode and Windows Virtual PC

> Get Windows XP Mode RC and Windows Virtual PC RC now

2 Select your system type (32-bit or 64-bit) and preferred language, then Download the installation files

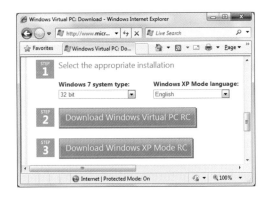

3 Double-click the downloaded Windows Virtual PC file to begin the installation

4 Accept the license agreement to apply the update to your Windows 7 system

5 Restart to complete the installation

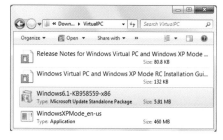

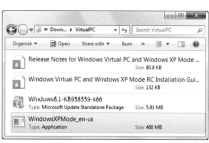

Windows Virtual PC will be added to the Start menu. However, the shortcuts that are added cannot be used until you set up a virtual machine.

To install Windows XP Mode:

1 Double-click the downloaded Windows XP Mode file to begin

2 Follow prompts to install the predefined virtual hard disk for Windows XP Mode

Don't forget

You can either use the Windows XP Mode feature, or create your own virtual machine.

123

Hot tip

When setup completes, the Windows XP Mode system will be launched, ready for configuration.

Configure XP Mode

Don't forget

To use Windows XP Mode, you must accept the terms of the license agreement.

1 When the virtual machine starts for the first time, accept the license agreement and click Next to continue

Hot tip

This is a default account set up with administrator privileges and used to run Windows XP mode.

2 Create a password for the account named XPMUser. Click Remember credentials to store the password

3 Configure Windows XP Mode for automatic updates, then the virtual system will be set up and initialized

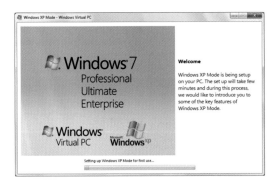

4 After Windows Virtual PC configures Windows XP Mode, the virtual machine starts up ready to use

You can now set up the Windows XP Mode system, using devices attached to your main Windows 7 system, including DVD drives, to install older applications like Paint Shop Pro v7 that need XP.

When you've installed the applications, you close down the Windows XP Mode virtual machine, and use the Windows 7 Start menu to access the virtual applications.

 1 Select Start, All Programs, Windows Virtual PC

 2 Select Windows XP Mode Applications, and click Jasc Software to locate Paint Shop Pro 7

 3 You can access any applications that have been installed for All Users on the XP system

Command Prompt

Windows includes an MS-DOS simulator in the form of the Command Prompt, which supports DOS commands and runs old DOS programs. To obtain the Command Prompt:

 Click Start, All Programs, Accessories and then select Command Prompt

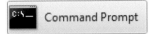

 Type MS-DOS commands at the command line. To display a list of commands and a brief description, type *Help* and press Enter

To set command prompt options, right-click the title bar and select Default (to change all Command Prompt Windows) or Properties (to make changes for just this one window)

Change the command prompt options as needed

When you have finished, click on the Close (X) button or type *Exit* and press the Enter key

...cont'd

You may need to select a specific folder to work with at the command prompt. You could use the MS-DOS commands to change folders. For example, to switch to user Harshad's Pictures folder you'd type: *cd c:\users\harshad\pictures*.

However, if the folder icon is visible on the screen, there's a quick way to open the Command Prompt ready switched to that folder:

1 Hold down Shift as you right-click the folder icon, then select from the extended menu the option to Open Command Window Here

2 The Command Prompt window appears, ready positioned at the required folder

Some commands will require administrator authority. To run these, open the Command Prompt as an administrator.

1 Click Start, All Programs, Accessories and then right-click Command Prompt and select Run as Administrator

Don't forget

The Open Command Window Here entry is hidden when you right-click the folder icon without pressing Shift.

Hot tip

The extended menu also provides the Copy as Path option which places the full path of the selected folder (or file) into the Clipboard.

Beware

This option will only be available for user accounts that have Administrator authority.

Task Manager

Task Manager lists all the programs and processes running on your computer, you can monitor performance or close a program that is no longer responding.

To open the Task Manager:

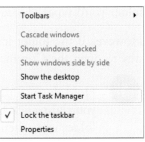

 Right-click an empty space on the Taskbar and select Task Manager, or press the key combination Ctrl+Shift+Esc

2 When Task Manager opens, click the Applications tab to see the active tasks

3 An application such as Paint Shop Pro running under Windows XP Mode is flagged Remote

4 If an application is given the status of Not Responding and you cannot wait for Windows to fix things, select the program and click End Task

 Click the Processes tab to show the system and the current user processes. Click the box Show processes from all users, if there are other user or guest accounts logged on

6 The total CPU usage and the amount being used by each process are shown as (continually varying) percentages

Click Performance to see graphs of resource usage

 The Performance panel shows graphs of the recent history of CPU and memory usage, along with other details

Alternative View

In addition to the standard view, with menus and tabs, Task Manager also has a CPU graph-only view.

1 To switch to the graph-only view double-click the graph area on the Performance tab

2 To switch back to the view with menus and tabs, double-click the graph area a second time

3 Click the Networking tab to view the activity on your local area network. This tab also offers a graph-only view

Resource Monitor

The Resource Monitor provides an even more detailed view of the activities on your computer, and can be an essential aid in troubleshooting. To start the Resource Monitor:

Hot tip

You could select Start, All Programs, Accessories, System Tools and select Resource Monitor.

1 From Task Manager, Performance tab click the Resource Monitor button

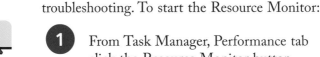

2 This displays CPU, Memory, Disk and Network details

Hot tip

Right-click any process and choose Analyze Wait Chain to see which tasks are holding up an unresponsive application.

3 For even more detail, select one of the tabs e.g. Memory

Don't forget

The Hardware Reserved section indicates how much of the 4GB maximum memory is unavailable to applications. With the 64-bit Windows 7, most of this memory would become accessible.

7 Internet and Windows

Set up a new Internet connection or link into your existing connection, then surf the net using the Internet Explorer web browser. Choose your preferred search engine, tabulate your favorite sites, take advantage of RSS (Really Simple Syndication) feeds and view multiple pages with tabbed browsing.

132 Internet Connection

134 Start Internet Explorer

136 Browse the Web

138 Browser Buttons

140 Search the Internet

141 Change Search Provider

142 Bookmark Favorites

143 RSS Feeds

144 History

145 Home Page

146 Tabbed Browsing

147 Zoom

148 Print

Internet Connection

Before you can use the Internet and browse the web, your computer needs to be set up for connection to the Internet. To do this you'll require:

- An Internet Service Provider (ISP), to provide an account that gives you access to the Internet

- A transmission network – cable, telephone or wireless

- Some hardware to link into that transmission network

- For a broadband connection, such as Digital Subscriber Line (DSL) or cable, you need a DSL or Cable modem or router, usually provided by the ISP

- For dial-up connection, you need a dial-up modem, which is usually pre-installed on your computer

Your ISP may provide software to help you set up your hardware, configure your system and register your ISP account details. However, if you are required to install the connection or, if you are configuring a second connection as a backup, you can use the Set Up a Connection or Network wizard.

 Click Start, Control Panel, View Network Status and Tasks (or in Icon View click Network and Sharing Center)

Network and Internet
View network status and tasks
Choose homegroup and sharing options

Network and Sharing Center

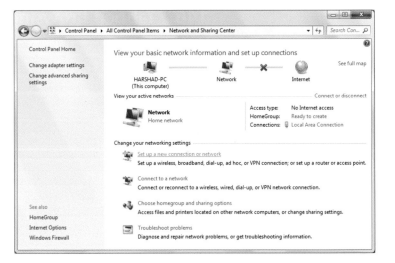

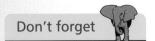

2 Click Setup a new connection or network to display the connection options supported

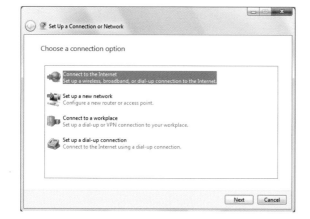

3 Select Connect to the Internet and click Next

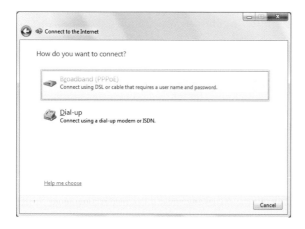

4 The Connect to the Internet wizard launches. Select the appropriate connection method from those offered

Windows identifies all of the possible connection methods based on the hardware configuration of your computer. If you have a wireless router or network, you may have an option for Wireless connection. If there's no dial-up modem installed in your computer, then the Dial-up connection method will not be offered.

133

Beware

If Windows has already recognized your connection, it detects this. You can select Browse the Internet now (see page 136) or set up a second connection (e.g. as a backup).

Don't forget

Continue through the wizard to complete the definition of your Internet connection, ready to start browsing the Internet.

Start Internet Explorer

Don't forget

When you search, you'll find Internet Explorer (No Add-ons), in Start, All Programs, Accessories, System Tools. This is a special troubleshooting version, for use when you have problems with particular websites.

Once your Internet connection has been set up, you can open Internet Explorer. There are a number of ways to do this:

1 Click the Internet Explorer icon on the Taskbar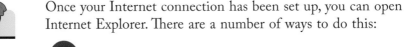

2 Select Start, All Programs then click Internet Explorer

3 Select Start, begin typing *internet explorer* and click Internet Explorer at the top of the Start menu

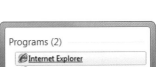

4 If you pin Internet Explorer to the Start menu (see page 114), you can click Start then select Internet Explorer

Whichever way you start Internet Explorer, for the first time, you'll be prompted to choose your preferred settings

1 Click Ask me later to postpone the choice

Hot tip

Suggested Sites displays sites similar to those you browse often, to help you discover more sites of interest. You can turn this on or off from the Favorites Center (see page 142).

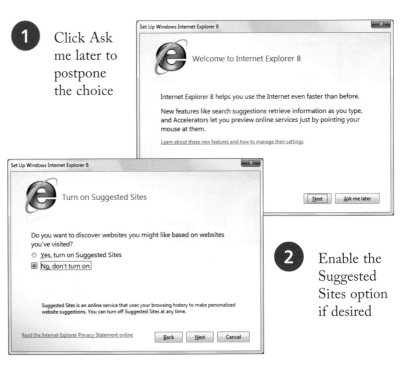

2 Enable the Suggested Sites option if desired

...cont'd

3 Accept the Express settings for recommended values, or choose Custom settings to review options individually

The Internet Explorer window shares the features described for Windows Explorer (see page 64), including the hidden Menu bar, but there are some differences and some extra items:

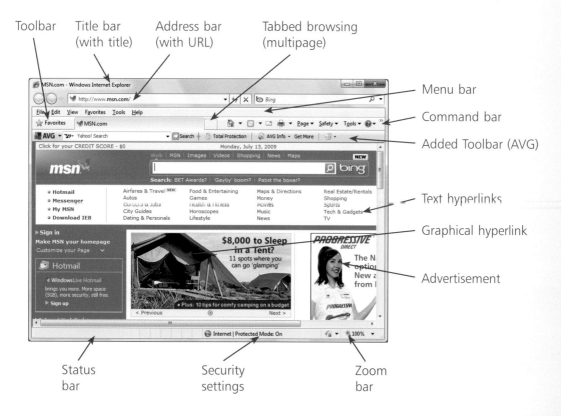

Toolbar · Title bar (with title) · Address bar (with URL) · Tabbed browsing (multipage)

Menu bar
Command bar
Added Toolbar (AVG)
Text hyperlinks
Graphical hyperlink
Advertisement

Status bar · Security settings · Zoom bar

Beware

Check which search engine is specified as the default when you use Express settings. Windows 7 specifies Microsoft's Bing (previously known as Windows Live Search). If you accept the express settings, you can revise or expand the choice later (see page 141).

135

Browse the Web

The World Wide Web (or Web for short) is an enormous collection of websites, each consisting of interconnected web pages. Every page on the web has a unique address, called a URL (Uniform Resource Locator) or simply a web address. You see these advertised everywhere – newspapers, magazines, television. The typical URL will look similar to this one:

http://www.microsoft.com/windows/default.mspx

web page indicator	server name	site type	sub section	web page

The server name is usually the company or organization name (in lower case), e.g. microsoft or ineasysteps.

The types of websites include:

- com   commercial and business
- org   organizations and charities
- edu   education and academic
- gov   government

There may also be a country suffix, for example:

- com.au   Australia
- ca   Canada
- co.uk   United Kingdom

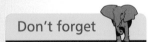
To visit the main web page for a company or organization, the server name and site type will usually be sufficient since default values for the remaining parts will be assumed. For example, to address the main website for Microsoft, the URL address required is www.microsoft.com. Note that the address gets extended to the default web page http://www.microsoft.com/en/us/default.aspx

...cont'd

To display a web page:

 Click in the Address bar and begin to type the URL of the web page you want to visit

As you type an address, Internet Explorer tries to finish it, based on web pages you've visited before. Continue typing until the page you want appears in the drop-down list, then click that entry.

 If no useful suggestion is offered, complete the address and click the Go To button or press Enter

Once you've reached a website, you can switch to another page, on the same site or on a different site, without typing a URL.

Move the mouse over a text or graphical hyperlink and the URL is displayed on the Status bar. Click to visit that address

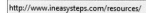

137

Hot tip

If you type just the name, e.g. *ineasysteps*, and press Ctrl+Enter, the www prefix and the .com suffix are added automatically, giving you www.ineasysteps.com.

Don't forget

When you move the mouse over a hyperlink, the link may change color and the mouse pointer will change to a hand symbol, indicating an associated web address.

Browser Buttons

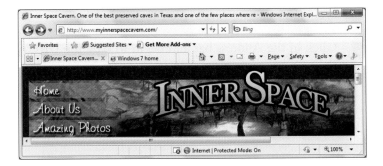

Don't forget

y default, there's no
enu bar displayed, and
olbar buttons have
een re-arranged to
ake functions readily
vailable.

The browser buttons that are provided include:

Back and Forward

Click the back and forward buttons to
switch between recently visited web pages,
or click the down arrow to select an entry
from the Recent Pages list

Hot tip

only the Favorites
utton is displayed,
ght-click it and select
avorites Bar to add the
ther buttons.

	Menu Bar
	Favorites Bar
	Compatibility View Button
✓	Command Bar
✓	Status Bar
	Windows Live Toolbar
	AVG Security Toolbar
	Lock the Toolbars
	Customize ▶

Quick Tabs and Tab List

Tabs allow you to view multiple web pages
in the same Internet Explorer window,

with the Quick Tabs button and the Tab List to let you switch
between pages, and the New Tab button to add more tabs.

The Address Bar

This includes the Go To, Refresh and Stop buttons
to control the loading of the web page specified in the address box

The Search Box

This provides the Search Options
button that allows you to select

your preferred search providers (see page 141)

Favorites Button and Favorites Bar

Don't forget

f you only have one tab
pen for display, Quick
abs and Tablist are
idden. See page 146
or details of Tabbed
rowsing.

The Favorites button displays the Favorites Center, with the
favorites, feeds and website history (see page 142). The Favorites
bar contains an initial two shortcuts, Suggested Sites and Get
More Add-ons, plus the Add to Favorites Bar button to include
further shortcuts.

...cont'd

The other browser buttons are included on the Command bar on the right. By default, the following nine buttons are enabled:

Home	Display the default Home web pages
Feeds	View or subscribe to RSS feeds on the page
Read Mail	Switch to the default email client
Print	Print web page (includes scaling to fit)
Page	Send page, send link, open in new window
Safety	InPrivate secure browsing and filtering
Tools	Pop up Blocker, Manage add-ons, Suggested sites
Help	Contents and Index, Tour, support, feedback
Blog This	Invoke Live Writer to create and publish a blog

To change the buttons available:

1 Right-click the Command bar and select Customize

2 Click Add or Remove Commands

The additional buttons available include:

A Text Size	Send Page by E-mail...
Encoding	Send Link by E-mail...
Edit	View Source
Cut	Webpage Privacy Policy...
Copy	Delete Browsing History...
Paste	Internet Options
Full Screen	Online Support
Developer Tools	Manage Add-ons
Print Preview...	SmartScreen Filter
Page Setup...	Pop-up Blocker
New Window	Zoom
Save As...	InPrivate Browsing

You can adjust the length of the Command bar, to show more buttons. If Lock the Toolbars is enabled (ticked), click to unlock, then drag the toolbar handle at the left.

You can Add or Remove commands, or Reset the Command bar to its original contents.

Search the Internet

If you are looking for something, but don't have a web address, use the Internet Explorer search features to locate likely pages.

1 Click in the Instant Search box and type a word or phrase related to the topic, then press Enter

| 🅱 chicago scoring for bridge | 🔍 | ▼ |

2 The search is completed using Bing search and the matching web pages are listed, with brief outlines

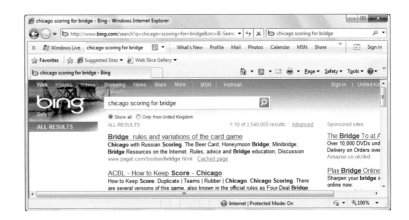

3 Click an entry to view the page. The Back button will return you to the Results list

Address Bar searches
The Address bar also operates as a search box.

1 In the Address bar, type *Find*, *Go* or *?* followed by the word or phrase and then press Enter and select the search suggestion or the web page redirection as appropriate

Change Search Provider

To add some new search providers to Internet Explorer:

 1 Click the down arrow at the right of the Search box, then click Find More Providers

2 The Internet Explorer search guide web page shows all the search providers supported

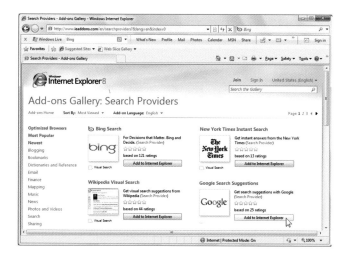

Hot tip

You can add extra search providers, for example Amazon and NYTimes, without making a change to the default and have them listed in Search options, ready for use when required.

141

3 Select a provider, for example, Google and click the box Make this my default search provider, if desired. Then click Add Provider

4 To choose a different search provider, just for the current session, click the arrow to open the Search options and select the one you want e.g. Wikipedia

5 To make further changes, click Manage Search Providers, choose any of the search providers and select Set as Default or Remove as appropriate

Hot tip

From Manage Search Providers, you can also enable or disable Search Suggestions for individual providers.

Bookmark Favorites

If you see a web page that you want to revisit, add it to your Favorites list to save having to record or remember the address.

Hot tip

You can also right-click any link in a web page or in search results, and select Add to Favorites.

 1 While viewing the page, click the Favorites button and then click the Add to Favorites button (or press Ctrl+D)

Don't forget

Click New Folder to define a subfolder, or click the down arrow to select an existing subfolder.

2 The page title is used as the name for the new favorite, but you can type an alternative name if you wish

3 Click Add to save the details in your Favorites list

View Favorites

1 Click the Favorites Center button and click the Favorites button (if not already selected)

2 Click on a folder name to expand it

3 Click any Favorites entry to display that web page

Hot tip

Click the green arrow to Pin the Favorites Center to the window, so you can explore multiple entries without redisplaying the Center. Press Close when you want it removed.

4 Click Add to Favorites and Organize Favorites, to move, rename or delete the entries

RSS Feeds

RSS (Really Simple Syndication) Feeds provide the frequently updated content from a news or blog website. Internet Explorer can discover and display feeds as you visit websites, or you can subscribe to feeds to automatically check for and download updates that you can view later.

Discover a Feed

1 Open Internet Explorer and browse to a website that has feeds, for example the CNN website (www.cnn.com). The Feeds button changes color to let you know

2 Click the arrow next to the Feeds button to see the list of feeds available

3 Click one of the feeds to view the contents and you are offered the opportunity to subscribe, so that feed updates will be automatically downloaded to your computer

4 Click Subscribe to this Feed, then click the Subscribe button, to add the feed to your list in the Favorites Center

Hot tip

If you click the Feed button, you'll select the first in the list (or the only feed if there's just one offered).

Hot tip

IE8 also supports Web slices. These are portions of a web page that you can subscribe to and view updates directly from the Favorites bar.

Don't forget

To view your subscribed feeds, click the Favorites Center button and then select the Feeds button.

143

History

1 Open the Favorites Center and click the History tab

Hot tip

You can also press Ctrl+H to open the Favorites Center at the History section.

2 Pin the Favorites Center to the window (see page 142), so you can browse the History entries

3 Click the down arrow on the bar below the History tab, to change the sort order for the entries

Manage the History

1 Select Tools, Internet Options and click the General tab

Don't forget

The general Internet Options also cover Home Page, Search, Tabs and appearance settings.

2 At Browsing History, click Delete to remove the records, or Settings to change the history period (default 20 days)

Home Page

Your home page is displayed when you start Internet Explorer or when you click the Home button. The web page displayed may be the Windows default, or may have been defined by your ISP or your computer supplier. However, you can choose any web page as your home page.

Current Web Page

 With the preferred web page displayed in the current tab, click the arrow next to the Home button and select Add or Change home page

Use this page as your only home page or add the page to your set of home pages

Hot tip

You can define all the open browser tabs as your home page.

Reset Home Page

Click Tools, Internet Options and click the General tab

Click Use Default to use the home page specified when you installed Internet Explorer

or

Click Use Blank to start up with no home page, e.g. when using the computer offline

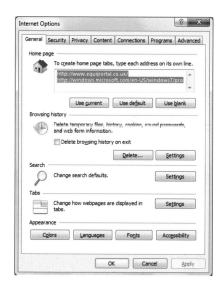

Don't forget

You can specify a new home page by typing the web address into the home page box.

Click OK to save the changes

Tabbed Browsing

You can open multiple websites in a single browser window, with each web page on a separate tab.

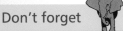

1 To open another tab, click the New Tab button

2 Type an address in the Address bar and press Enter

3 To switch between tabs, click the page tab on the tab row or click the Quick Tabs button and select the page

4 Close Internet Explorer and you'll be asked if you want to Close all tabs or just Close current tab

5 You can Reopen closed tabs from a new tab, next time you start Internet Explorer

Zoom

Internet Explorer Zoom allows you to enlarge or reduce your view of a web page. Unlike the Text Size button (see page 139), it enlarges everything on the page (image and text).

 Click the Zoom button to view the page at 125%, 150% or 100% (for each click it selects the next value)

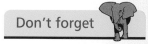

 Click the down arrow to select one of the predefined zoom levels (for example, 400%)

Hot tip

Reduce (zoom out) to get an overall view of a large web page. Enlarge (zoom in) to see the fine detail for one section of the page.

Don't forget

Click Custom to specify a magnification factor from 10% to 1000%.

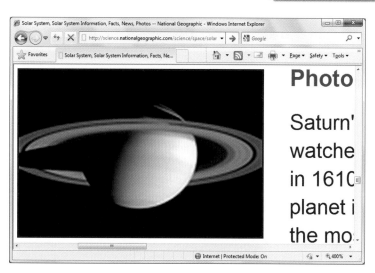

 Click the Zoom button once, to return to 100%

Wheel Mouse Zoom

 If you have a wheel mouse, hold down Ctrl and scroll the wheel to zoom in or out

Keyboard Zoom

1 Press Ctrl – to reduce, or Ctrl + to enlarge, in 25% increments. Press Ctrl + * to return to 100%

Print

 Click the Print button on the Command bar, and Internet Explorer automatically prints the current tab

Use Print Preview to see how the printed web page will appear.

 With the required web page open, click the arrow next to the print button and select Print Preview

 Note that the Shrink to Fit option is preselected in the Change Print Size box

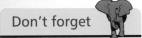 To illustrate the benefit of this, click the down arrow and select 100% and see how the print width gets truncated

8 Email and Messaging

Windows allows you to send and receive email messages online, using Internet Explorer on any computer. You can also use Windows Live Mail to download your email messages on your own computer, and use Windows Live Messenger to send and receive instant messages.

150 Web Mail

152 Enable Pop Mail

153 Start Windows Live Mail

155 Receive Emails

156 Read a Message

157 Reply to a Message

158 Compose a New Message

159 Windows Live Contacts

160 Instant Messaging

162 Newsgroups

164 Block Spam Senders

166 Send a Web Page

Web Mail

Web Mail stores and retains your email on a mail server. To access your messages, you connect to the Internet and use Internet Explorer (or another web browser).

Hot tip

To send or receive email, you use your browser for Web Mail (web- or Internet-based), or the downloadable Windows Live Mail for POP (Post Office Protocol) mail (see page 152).

1 Open Internet Explorer and visit the website for your web mail provider, e.g. www.gmail.com

2 Provide your account name (usually your email ID or the full email address) and your password, then click Sign in

Don't forget

The main web mail services are particularly subject to spam messages, although the service provider will usually detect and transfer such messages into a separate folder.

3 You'll see a list of headers with details such as sender, subject and date or time

4 The paperclip icon indicates that there are files attached

5 Double-click a message header to open it, enabling the contents of the message to be retrieved from the server and displayed. The message remains on the server, unless you explicitly delete it

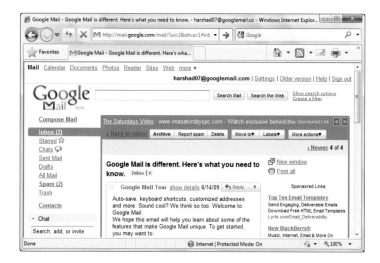

Hot tip

To delete messages, click in the boxes to select the messages, then click the Delete button to remove them from the server.

As a result, the messages can be viewed again, from any computer connected to the Internet. This is very useful if you want to check mail from other locations, for example, at an Internet cafe while on vacation, from a laptop and from a desktop computer.

The disadvantage is that you must be connected to the Internet and signed on to the email account, for any actions involving messages. The retrieval process may also be time consuming.

POP Mail

POP Mail also stores messages on the mail server, but when you retrieve your mail, using Windows Live Mail (or another email application), the messages are transferred from the server to the computer issuing the request. When the transfer is completed, the messages are deleted from the server.

You will be able to read messages and compose replies without having to be connected to the Internet. You may also have functions and features that are not available via web mail, such as message or diary management. Message access will often be much faster. However, once you have downloaded your mail, you must have access to that computer to view the messages again.

Hot tip

Most web mail providers have a POP mail facility, so you can use both methods with the same account. However, in some cases there may be a charge for this service. Similarly, your ISP may provide web access to your POP email account.

Enable Pop Mail

If your email account is web-based, like the Gmail accounts from Google, your messages are stored on the mail server, managed by your email service supplier. This means you must always be online to read your messages. However, you may be able to change the settings for the account so that you can download your messages and store them on your computer, using the POP mail function. This requires an application such as Windows Mail for Vista or Windows Live Mail for Windows 7.

To enable POP in your Gmail account:

1 Log in to your Gmail account and click Settings at the top of the web page

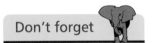

2 Click the Forwarding and POP tab in Mail Settings

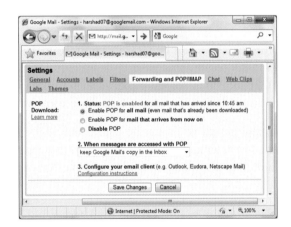

Beware

This step will not be necessary for email accounts provided as a POP service by your ISP.

Don't forget

Gmail also supports email forwarding and the use of an Imap server instead of a POP server to access your email via Windows Live Mail.

3 Select Enable POP for all mail (to download existing messages) or Enable POP for mail that arrives from now on

4 Choose what action to take with Gmail messages after they are accessed with POP, then click Save Changes

Your preferences have been saved.

Start Windows Live Mail

Windows Live Mail provides the tools that you require in order to send and receive email messages using the POP mail method.

To start Windows Live Mail:

 Click Start, All Programs, Windows Live and then select the Windows Live Mail entry

> Startup
> Windows Live
>   Windows Live Call
>   Windows Live Family Safety
>   Windows Live Mail
>   Windows Live Messenger
>   Windows Live Movie Maker Beta
>   Windows Live Photo Gallery
>   Windows Live Writer

Windows Live Mail

© 2009 Microsoft Corporation. All rights reserved. This program is protected by U.S. and international copyright laws as described in the help/about box.

The first time you start Windows Live Mail, it will prompt you for your email account details, beginning with your email address, password and preferred display name

Add an E-mail Account

Please enter your e-mail account information below:

E-mail address: harshad07@googlemail.com
example555@hotmail.com   Get a free e-mail account

Password: ●●●●●●●●
☑ Remember password

How should your name appear in e-mail sent from this account?

Display Name: Harshad Kotecha
For example: John Smith

☑ Manually configure server settings for e-mail account

Next   Cancel

Select the box Manually configure server settings for email account, so you can provide the details

Click Next to continue

Hot tip

Previous versions of Windows provided Outlook Express or Windows Mail to support the email functions. In Windows 7 you'll need to download Windows Live Mail from the Windows Live website (see page 33).

Don't forget

The email service provider may offer an automatic method for defining your account details to the email program, to save you entering the details manually.

Hot tip

Click the box to ask Windows Live Mail to remember the password, so you don't have to enter it each time you send or receive mail.

...cont'd

5 Specify the incoming and outgoing email servers for your service provider. For Gmail, you'd put:

6 Note that Port numbers 965 and 465 must be specified for the incoming and outgoing server respectively

7 You must also specify that the server requires a secure connection (SSL) and that the outgoing server will require authentication when sending mail

8 Set this account as the default then click Finish

Receive Emails

1 Windows Live Mail starts up and downloads the email messages available for the new account

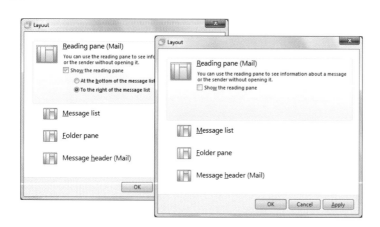

Don't forget

You must be connected to the Internet, by dial-up or by broadband, in order to be able to send or receive messages.

2 Note that the currently selected message will be displayed in the Reading pane, and marked as read

3 To switch off the Reading pane, select View and click Layout

4 Clear the box that is labeled Show the reading pane

Beware

The message that is automatically selected and displayed could turn out to be spam, so it might be better to avoid using the preview pane.

155

Hot tip

Layout also allows you to adjust the view for the Message list, the Folder pane and the Message header.

Read a Message

Downloaded messages are stored in your Inbox. The sender, the title and the date/time sent are displayed along with icons that indicate the status of the messages:

The closed yellow envelope indicates an Unread message

The open white envelope indicates a Read message

The paperclip icon indicates a file Attachment

The red exclamation mark is for a High priority message

The blue down arrow indicates a Low priority message

The flag identifies a message needing attention later

1 Select the Inbox folder and the message you want to read, then press Enter or double-click the message header

2 The message opens in its own window. Scroll through the message (if necessary) to see all the content

Reply to a Message

It is easy to respond to any email message that you receive.

1 With the message open, click the Reply button to send an answer to the originator

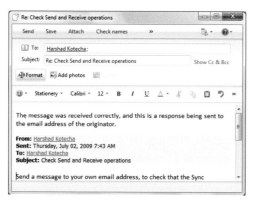

Hot tip

Click Reply All to send the message to all recipients of the email, as well as to the originator. Click Forward to share the message with other users.

2 Note the Re: prefix added to the message subject. Type your response above the original text message text

3 Click the File Attachment button, the Check Names or one of the Priority buttons, as appropriate

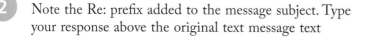

4 Click the Send button, and the reply will be placed in the Outbox from where it will be uploaded

157

Don't forget

If you are connected to the Internet, the reply message will be sent immediately and then transferred from the Outbox to the Sent Items folder. If you are offline, replies will be sent the next time you press Sync.

Hot tip

The envelope icons are modified to show that a response to the message has been sent, or that the message has been forwarded.

Compose a New Message

1 With the Mail folder selected, click the New button to open a plain message form

New ▾

Or from any other area, e.g. Calendar, click the down arrow next to New and select Email Message

New ▾	
Event	Ctrl+Shift+E
Calendar	Ctrl+Shift+D
E-mail message	Ctrl+N
Photo e-mail	Ctrl+Shift+P
News message	Ctrl+Shift+W
Contact	Ctrl+Shift+N

Or press the keys Ctrl+N

2 A fresh message form is displayed

158

3 Start typing a recipient name, then click the Check Names button. The associated email address will be displayed for you to select

4 Enter additional names as required, then enter your message and send it to the selected recipients (as described for a reply to a message, see page 157)

Windows Live Contacts

1 Open a Windows Live Mail message from the particular person or group, and right-click the sender name

Hot tip

You can use your Windows Live Contacts to store the names, email addresses, and other information about the people and organizations you communicate with.

2 Click Add Contact next to Sender, enter any additional details that you have, e.g. phone number, mailing address and even a photograph or image, then click the Add Contact button

Don't forget

Right-click an email address and select Add to contacts, to add addressees from the To: list and the Cc: list. If an email address is already in your Contacts folder, you get a message to that effect.

3 To open your Windows Live Contacts, select Contacts from the folder list in the Folders pane

Hot tip

If the Folder shortcuts are collapsed, then click the Contacts button.

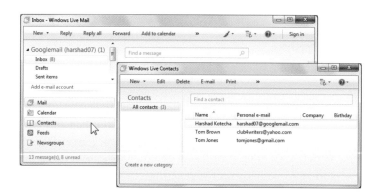

159

Instant Messaging

If the people you want to communicate with are online, you can send messages directly to them without needing email, using the instant messaging facilities offered by Windows Live Messenger.

When you download and install the Windows Live Essentials (see page 33) you'll be asked to sign in to Windows Live Messenger.

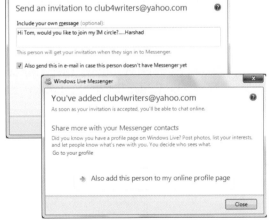

1 Provide your Windows Live ID and password

2 Specify your status and if desired ask Windows to remember ID and password

3 Ask Windows Live Messenger to sign you in automatically when Windows starts up

4 Select Add a contact and provide the instant messaging address or email address and send an invitation

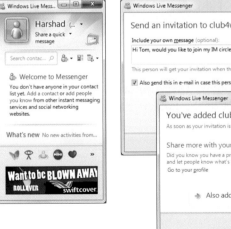

5 When your invitation is accepted, your contact will be added to your instant messaging circle

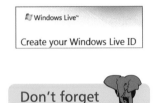
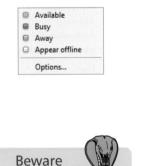

6 Windows Live Messenger shows your Instant Messaging circle and the status for your contacts

7 Click the Add button to add contacts, groups and categories, or to search for people

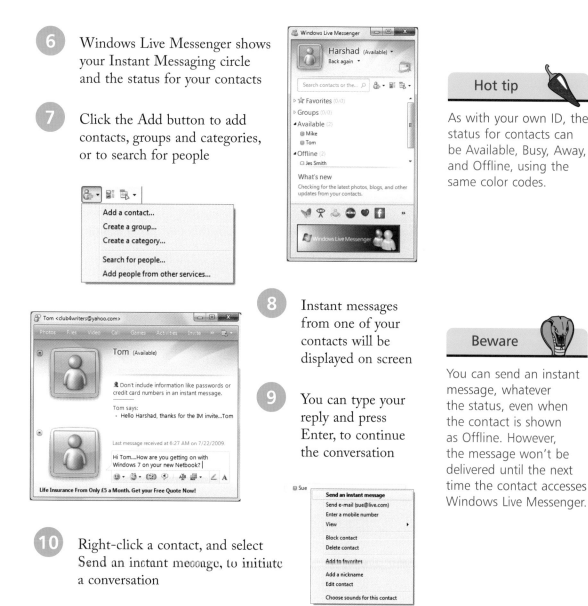

Add a contact...
Create a group...
Create a category...

Search for people...
Add people from other services...

8 Instant messages from one of your contacts will be displayed on screen

9 You can type your reply and press Enter, to continue the conversation

10 Right-click a contact, and select Send an instant message, to initiate a conversation

Send an instant message
Send e-mail (sue@live.com)
Enter a mobile number
View
Block contact
Delete contact
Add to favorites
Add a nickname
Edit contact
Choose sounds for this contact

11 You can add your contacts from other services such as Facebook or MySpace

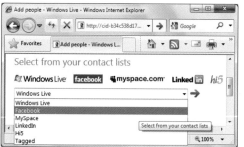

Newsgroups

Newsgroups require a newsreader program to download messages from a news server. This function is not included in Windows 7 itself, but is provided by Windows Live Mail. Your ISP may provide news servers, and there are many private news servers and newsgroups that require an account name and password for access. There's also a predefined link to the Microsoft newsgroups.

1 Open Windows Live Mail and select Newsgroups from the Folders

2 Click View Newsgroups, and the list of newsgroups available is downloaded, in this case many hundreds

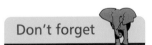
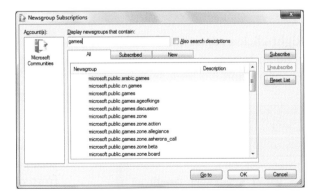

3 Type a term to focus the list onto your area of interest

4 Select a newsgroup and click Go To, to view its contents

Subscribe to a newsgroup

It can be tedious to search for newsgroups to check for the latest
updates, so it may be worth subscribing to particular newsgroups.
These will then be available on the Windows Live Mail folder list,
and you can have the latest messages downloaded automatically.

 1 Locate newsgroups that you are interested in, using
appropriate search keywords

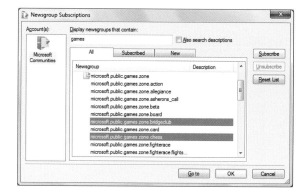

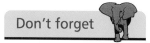
Don't forget

A folder icon will appear
next to any newsgroups
you have subscribed to.

2 Click one or more newsgroups and then click Subscribe

3 When you've added all the newsgroups you want, click
OK and messages for the selected newsgroups are shown

Hot tip

To subscribe to more
than one newsgroup,
press the Ctrl key, then
click the remaining
newsgroups you want.

4 You can synchronize all
messages, new messages only
or message headers only

Beware

Not all the newsgroups
listed have conversations
in progress, so you may
find some that have no
messages to display.

Block Spam Senders

Windows Live Mail helps you to keep your Inbox free of unsolicited commercial email messages (spam) by moving them to the Junk Email folder.

To specify the level of protection from spam that you require:

1 Click the Menus button to the right of the toolbar and then select the Safety options

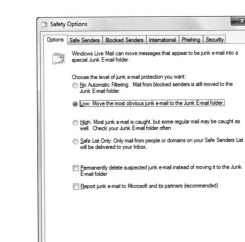

2 Choose No Automatic Filtering to stop blocking junk email messages. However, Windows Live Mail still blocks messages from locations on your Blocked Senders list

3 Low blocks only the most obvious junk email and is sufficient if your account isn't particularly subject to spam

4 High may be necessary, if you receive a large volume of junk email messages

5 The Safe List Only is the most restrictive. You only receive messages from people or domain names on your Safe Senders list

If a legitimate email message has been blocked:

1 Open Windows Live Mail, click the Junk email folder, select the message that was incorrectly classified

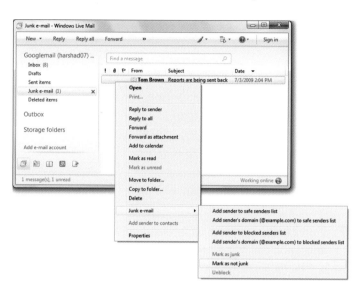

2 Right-click the message and select Junk Email then Mark as Not Junk. The message is moved to the Inbox

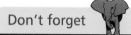

3 To prevent future problems, add the Sender to the Safe Senders List, using the same Junk Email menu

4 In a similar fashion, when a spam message gets through to the Inbox, right-click the message and choose Add Sender to Blocked Senders List

When you add a sender to the one list it will automatically be removed from the other list, if present. However, conflicts can arise. For example, if you add a domain name to one list, and an individual address from that domain to the other list.

Send a Web Page

Don't forget

If you come across a web page that has information you'd like to share with others, you can send the contents in an email message.

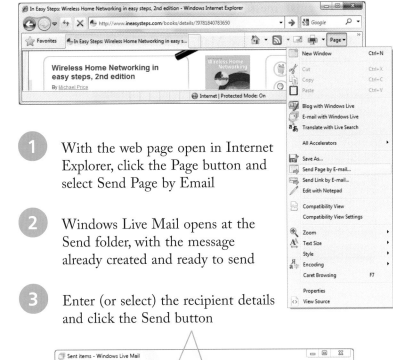

1 With the web page open in Internet Explorer, click the Page button and select Send Page by Email

2 Windows Live Mail opens at the Send folder, with the message already created and ready to send

3 Enter (or select) the recipient details and click the Send button

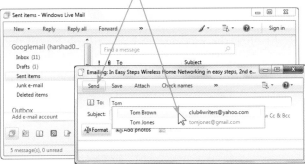

Hot tip

You could also select Send Link by Email from the Page menu, and the recipient will get a smaller message with the URL as the contents.

Send Page by E-mail...
Send Link by E-mail...

4 The message containing the web page details will be sent

9 Networking

There is a built-in networking capability within Windows, allowing you to share files, printers and your Internet connection between two or more computers, creating a HomeGroup between Windows 7 systems.

168 Network Components

169 Set Up Your Network

170 Internet Connection

172 Discover Networks

173 Network and Sharing Center

174 Join the HomeGroup

176 Sharing a Printer

177 Network Map

178 View Network Components

179 Share Files and Folders

180 Network Troubleshooting

Network Components

There are numerous possibilities for setting up a home network. To start with, there are two major network technologies:

● Wired – e.g. Ethernet, using twisted pair cables, to send data at rates of 10, 100 or 1000 Mbps (megabits per second)

● Wireless – using radio waves to send data at rates of 11 or 54 Mbps (or up to 300 Mbps with the latest devices)

There is also a variety of hardware items needed:

● Network adapter – appropriate to the network type, with one for each computer in the network

● Network controller – one or more hub, switch or router, providing the actual connection to each network adapter

Internet   Modem
Ethernet
Adapters
Wireless
Adapters   Router

There's also the Internet connection (dial-up, DSL or cable) using:

● A modem connected to one of the computers

● A modem connected to the network

● Internet access incorporated into the router or switch

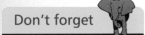

Don't forget

The network adapter can be connected to the USB port, inserted in the PC Card slot or installed inside your computer.

Don't forget

Ethernet adapters connect to a network hub, switch or wired router. Wireless adapters connect through a wireless router or a combination of router/switch.

Hot tip

You may already have some of these elements in operation, if you have an existing network running a previous version of Windows.

Set Up Your Network

The steps you'll need, and the most appropriate sequence to follow, will depend on the specific options on your system. However, the main steps will include:

- Install network adapters in the computers, where necessary

- Set up or verify the Internet connection

- Configure the wireless router or access point

- Connect other computers and start up Windows on each PC

Install Hardware
If you need to install a wired or wireless network adapter, follow the instructions provided with the adapter. For example, to install the Linksys Wireless-N USB adapter:

 Insert the CD provided and the setup program will start up automatically. Select the Click Here to Start button

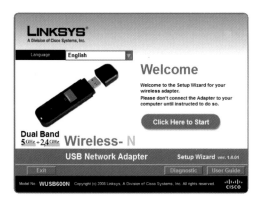

2 Follow the instructions (giving permission for access where requested) to complete the software installation

3 When prompted, attach the adapter to a USB port, via a cable if needed

4 When Windows has detected the wireless networks in your neighborhood, select your network and click the Connect button

Hot tip

With all the options and combinations that might be available, configuring the network could be complex. However, Windows 7 is designed to automate as much of the task as possible.

Don't forget

Depending on the AutoPlay settings, you may be prompted to run the installation program when you insert the CD.

169

Beware

Enter the security key for your wireless network when prompted.

Don't forget

If your router has been installed, Windows will automatically complete the connection to the Internet.

Beware

If you go to a website that stays relatively static, some of its web pages might be stored on your computer and will display correctly even if your connection is faulty.

Internet Connection

You don't actually require an Internet connection to set up a network, if all you want to do is share files and printers. However, in most cases the main purpose of the network is to share your connection to the Internet across several computers.

Verify your Connection

If you already have an Internet connection, open your web browser and go to a website that gets regularly updated (e.g. a news site). If the website opens with up-to-date entries and you don't get any error messages your connection is working.

Install Router

You can use a router with a DSL modem (an Internet gateway) to make an Internet connection available for sharing. This is usually set up on one computer, connected via an Ethernet cable or a USB cable. A configuration program may be provided on an installation CD or you can use your web browser.

1 Open the browser and enter the IP address provided for the router, e.g. 192.168.1.254 or a similar local IP address

2 Select Settings and enter the administrator user name (if required) and password, as provided by your ISP

You'll be using the default ID and password for the particular equipment. While this can only be accessed from a direct local connection, you may feel more secure if you change the password.

3 Select Admin Password, then enter the old password and the new password and click to Change password

Don't forget

The options offered will depend on the particular features of your router or gateway device, but they should be similar in principle.

4 Select Wireless to change the setup, for example by providing a new SSID (Service Set Identifier, the wireless network name) and choosing the encryption type and key

Beware

Do not use the default values for the parameters since these could be known to other people.

5 You can also change the channels used for the wireless communications, if you have problems with network range or speed, or interference from other devices

Discover Networks

Connect your computers to form your network, using Ethernet cables and adapters or by setting up your wireless adapters and routers. When you start up each of the computers, Windows 7 will examine the current configuration and discover any new networks that have been established since the last start up.

1 When a new network is detected, Windows asks you the location type – Home, Work or Public Location

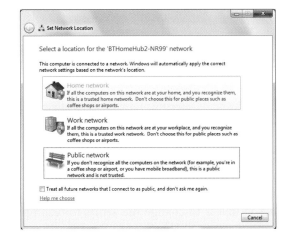

2 If you select Home network, Windows 7 will offer to create a HomeGroup to share files and printers

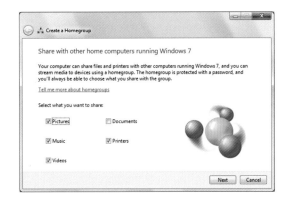

3 Choose the types of files and devices that you want to share over your home network, then click Next and Finish

Network and Sharing Center

1 To open the Network and Sharing Center, select Start, Control Panel and click View network status and tasks

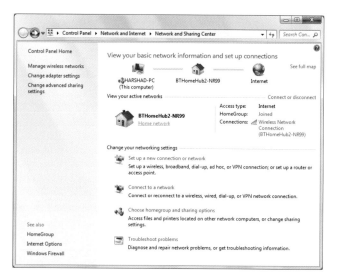

Don't forget

The Network and Sharing Center displays network settings and provides access to networking tasks for the computer.

Hot tip

Click the current network location, in this case Home Network to change to a different network location.

173

2 Click the network icon to change the network name

3 Click the Change button to select a different icon for the network, then click OK to confirm changes

Beware

Using a different network name on some of the computers on your local network makes it slower to complete the network discovery process.

Join the HomeGroup

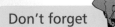
When you add a PC to your network, Windows on that computer will detect that there is a HomeGroup already created.

1 Open the Network and Sharing Center on the new PC

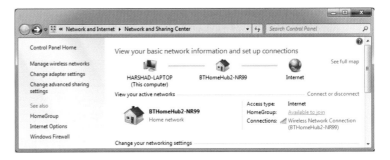

2 Click the HomeGroup link Available to join

174

Don't forget

Only computers on the same Home network and running the Windows 7 operating system (any edition) will be invited to join the HomeGroup.

3 Confirm the network creation details, and click Join Now

4 Specify shared items

5 Click Next

6 Enter the password that was specified for the HomeGroup when it was created

Don't forget

Windows generates the password when the HomeGroup is created (see page 172). If you forget the password, you can find it in the Control Panel on any computer already joined to the HomeGroup.

7 Click Next to validate the password

8 You have now joined the HomeGroup, so click Finish

When you check in the Network and Sharing Center for the new computer, you'll see the HomeGroup is now Joined, and you can access the files and printers that are available on the HomeGroup.

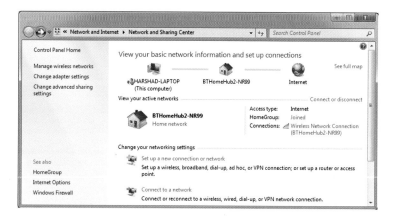

Hot tip

If there's a printer to be shared, Windows will automatically take the action needed to make it available on the network (see page 176).

Sharing a Printer

When you join the HomeGroup, Windows may detect a shared printer. However, the software drivers required may not be installed on this machine. To make the printer available:

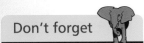
Don't forget

When you join the HomeGroup on your network, Windows will identify any additional actions needed, such as installing printer drivers.

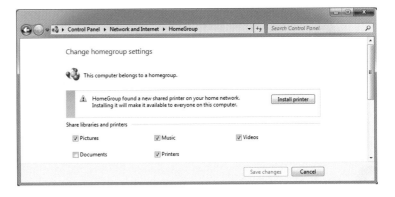

1 Click the button labelled Install printer

Hot tip

To view the printers on the computer, select Start, and click the Devices and Printers entry on the Start menu.

2 Click Install driver, to confirm you trust the computer and network sharing the printer, and the files are copied

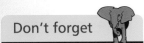
Don't forget

If Devices and Printers doesn't appear on the Start menu, select Start, Control Panel and click View devices and printers.

Hardware and Sound
View devices and printers
Add a device
Connect to a projector
Adjust commonly used mobility settings

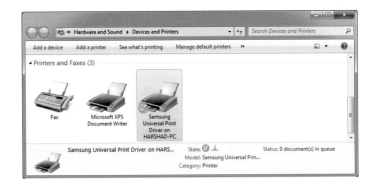

3 The shared printer is added to the Devices and Printers

Network Map

1 From the Network and Sharing Center click View Full Map to see a schematic diagram of the network

Don't forget

Computers running operating systems other than Windows, may not appear on the map.

2 Windows detects the available network segments, in this case Wireless and Ethernet, and creates the map

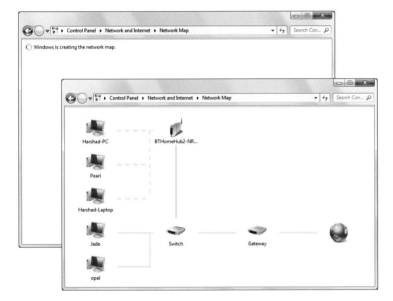

Hot tip

The dashed lines show the Wireless segment, while the solid lines show the Ethernet segment. The Router is shown as two components (Access Point and Gateway).

177

3 Hold the mouse pointer over a network device icon for details, including the IP address assigned to it

4 The details offered depend on the device type. Windows XP computers for example support only IPv4

Hot tip

Windows Vista and Windows 7 computers show similar information, but the details differ for other devices.

View Network Components

You can also view the network components in the Network folder.

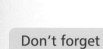
1 Open the Network and Sharing Center and click the Network icon

BTHomeHub2-NR99

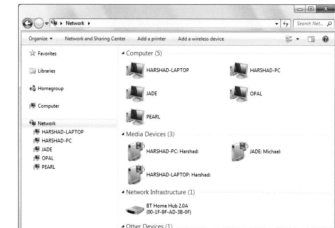

2 To view the shared items offered by a particular computer, for example the Harshad-PC, double-click the associated icon

HARSHAD-PC

3 Double-click the User Share to show the folders that are being shared

Public files and folders plus those belonging to the currently active user are available for access.

Share Files and Folders

1 Open the drive and right-click the folder to be shared

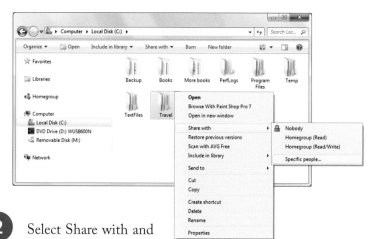

2 Select Share with and then a HomeGroup option, or select Specific people to share with

179

3 Add the user names that are required and click Share

Network Troubleshooting

1 Open the Network and Sharing Center and select Troubleshoot problems

 Troubleshoot problems
Diagnose and repair network problems, or get troubleshooting information.

2 Windows searches online for troubleshooting packs

3 Select for example Shared Folders and follow the prompts to describe and hopefully resolve your problems

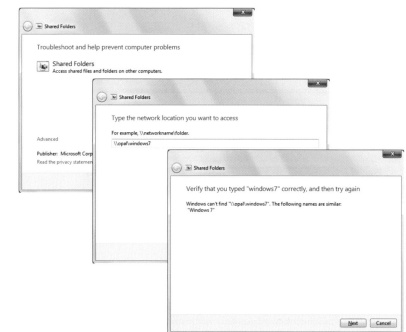

10 Customize Windows

This chapter shows you how to change your Windows 7 desktop and alter other settings to suit your requirements. It introduces Aero themes that apply a set of adjustments in one step. You can create new user accounts and customize each one individually and even create a password reset disk to be sure you can sign on.

182 Personalize Your Computer

184 Change Color and Sound

186 Screen Saver

187 Get More Themes

188 Windows 7 Basic

189 Desktop Icons

190 Screen Resolution

191 Display Settings

192 Desktop Gadgets

194 User Accounts

196 Configure the Account

197 Password Reset Disk

198 Date and Time Functions

200 Ease of Access Center

202 Mouse Settings

Personalize Your Computer

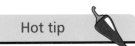

There are several ways to display the personalization options in Windows 7:

1 Right-click the desktop and select the Personalize entry

2 Select Start, Control Panel and, with View by Icons selected, double-click the Personalization button

3 With the default Control Panel View by Category, select Appearance and Personalization and then select the Personalization option

4 The Personalization options for your system are displayed

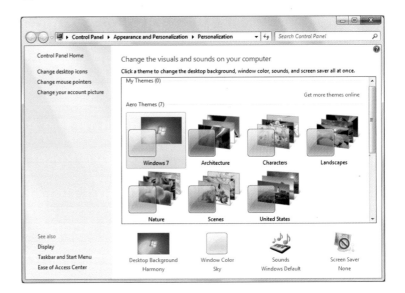

The functions offered depend on the edition of Windows 7 you have installed and the hardware specifications of your PC. The illustration above is from a system with Ultimate edition and with an Aero-compatible display adapter.

1 Select one of the Aero Themes offered, e.g. Landscapes and Scenes or your location-specific theme

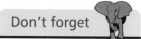
2 Choosing United States for example replaces the standard Windows 7 theme with a slide show of related images

3 Click the Desktop Background button to select your own pictures for the slide show

Change Color and Sound

1 Open Personalization and click the Windows Color button

Beware

The Windows Color option is displayed for the Windows Aero scheme only. The Classic and 7 Basic schemes, have just the Appearance Settings dialog shown below.

2 With any of the Aero Themes active, the Windows Color and Appearance selection dialog box is displayed

3 Choose one of the predefined colors to change the color for windows, the Start menu and the taskbar

Don't forget

You can adjust the level of transparency, and you can also create a custom color using the sliders in the color mixer.

4 Click Advanced appearance settings for Windows Color and Appearance, used for non-Aero settings

5 Make adjustments to the settings then click OK to apply them or click Cancel to exit without saving the changes

Select Sounds from Personalization, to see the name of the sound theme that gets applied to events in Windows

Sounds

Don't forget

Click the down-arrow on the Sound Scheme bar to try out a different scheme.

Hot tip

If you do not want to have sounds associated with Windows events, select the sound scheme No Sounds.

185

 Select an event such as Windows Logoff and click the Test button to hear the associated sound

 Browse to locate a new sound file (file type .wav), then click Test to preview the effect

 Make any other changes, then click Save As, and provide a name for your modified sound scheme

Screen Saver

With the Screen Saver enabled, when your mouse or keyboard has been idle for a specified period of time, Windows will display a moving image or pattern. To specify the image used:

1 From Personalization, click the Screen Saver button (which initially shows None for themes provided with Windows 7)

2 Click the Screen Saver bar and choose a screen saver e.g. Mystify

3 Click the Preview button to check out the action

4 Set the time delay after which the screen saver will be invoked, and choose to display the logon screen when the system resumes

5 Click OK to put the screen saver or settings into effect

Personalization will now show the name of the Screen Saver that has been enabled.

Get More Themes

You can download more Windows 7 themes:

1 Open Personalization and select Get more themes online

Don't forget

This shows a sample theme and a sample background, and also offers advice on how to create your own themes and share them with other people.

2 Scroll down to find the collection of themes

Hot tip

Click the Download button to install the associated theme. You can still switch themes using personalization.

3 Click the Desktop backgrounds tab to see the selection

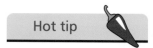

Hot tip

Click Download to open the associated picture then right-click the image and select Set as Background.

Windows 7 Basic

To use the Aero themes and other Aero features, your computer must have a suitable display adapter. This is an example that fails:

Beware

If the video adapter isn't of the appropriate type, the Windows 7 Basic theme will be applied when the operating system is installed.

Don't forget

Windows notes that there was a problem with transparency and other Aero effects.

 Click the Troubleshoot problems annotation and follow the prompts to detect problems with the display adapter

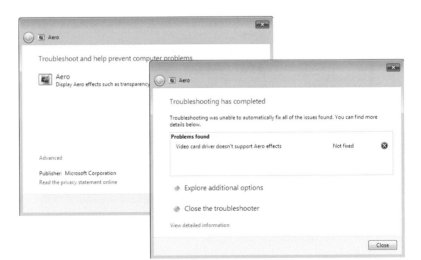

Hot tip

The adapter concerned was a 16MB ATi Rage Ultra which is well below the requirements for Aero effects.

 The troubleshoot report confirms that there are issues with the display adapter and its driver software

Desktop Icons

To control the display of icons on the desktop:

 Right-click the desktop, click View and select Show Desktop Icons. A check mark is added

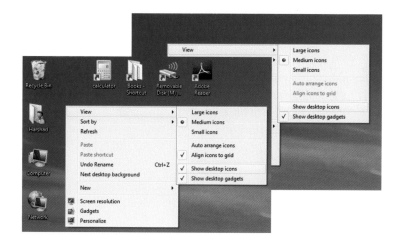

Hot tip

There are system icons that can be displayed on the desktop, the programs you install may add icons there, and you can also create shortcuts (see page 113).

 To resize the icons, display the View menu as above and click Large Icons, Medium Icons or Small Icons

 To remove the check mark and hide all the icons, display the View menu and click Show Desktop Icons again

 To choose which of the system icons appear, open Personalization and select Change Desktop Icons

Don't forget

You can use the scroll wheel on your mouse to resize desktop icons. On the desktop, hold down Ctrl as you roll the wheel up or down.

189

 Select or clear the boxes to show or hide icons as required

Beware

Windows 7 Starter Edition does not have Personalization, but you can select Start, type *common*, and select Show or hide common icons on the desktop.

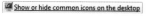
Show or hide common icons on the desktop

Screen Resolution

If you have a high resolution screen, you may find that the text as well as the icons are too small. You can increase the effective size by reducing the screen resolution.

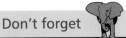

Don't forget

This menu is available in all editions of Windows including Starter edition.

1 Right-click a clear section of desktop and select Screen Resolution

2 Alternatively Select Start, Control Panel, Appearance and Personalization and click Adjust screen resolution

View	▶
Sort by	▶
Refresh	
Paste	
Paste shortcut	
New	▶
Screen resolution	
Gadgets	
Personalize	

Appearance and Personalization
Change the theme
Change desktop background
Adjust screen resolution

Change the appearance of your display

Detect
Identify

Display: 1. Mobile PC Display ▼
Resolution: 1920 × 1200 (recommended) ▼
Orientation: Landscape ▼

Advanced settings

Connect to a projector (or press the ∎ key and tap P)
Make text and other items larger or smaller
What display settings should I choose?

OK Cancel Apply

Beware

If you have an LCD monitor or a laptop computer, you are recommended to stay with the native resolution, normally the highest. To resize text and icons in this case, you would adjust the DPI (see opposite page).

3 Click the down arrow next to Resolution and drag the slider, then click Apply

4 Click the down arrow next to Orientation to switch the view to Portrait e.g. for tablet PCs

Landscape ▼
Landscape
Portrait
Landscape (flipped)
Portrait (flipped)

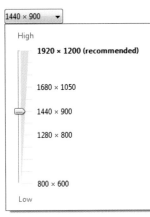

1440 × 900 ▼

High
1920 × 1200 (recommended)
1680 × 1050
1440 × 900
1280 × 800
800 × 600
Low

Display Settings

1 Select Start, Control Panel, Appearance and Personalization and then click Display

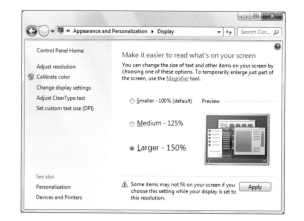

Don't forget

You can change your display settings and make it easier to read what's on the screen.

2 Select for example Larger – 150%, and click Apply

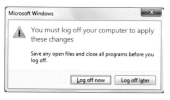

3 Logoff so that the change can take effect, then logon

Don't forget

Select Set custom text size, and drag the ruler to set any value between 100% and 500%.

9 point Segoe

191

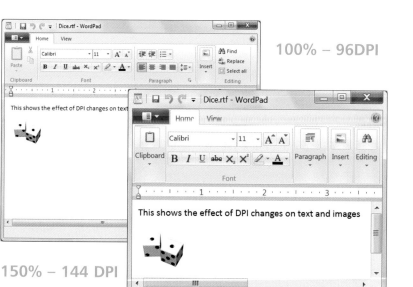

100% – 96DPI

150% – 144 DPI

This shows the effect of DPI changes on text and images

Hot tip

The WordPad screenshots illustrate how the text, icons and images are all proportionally resized when you change the DPI setting.

Desktop Gadgets

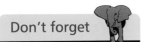

Don't forget

There are ten gadgets in Windows 7, including Calendar, Clock, CPU Meter, Currency, Feed Headlines, Media Center, Picture Puzzle, Slide Show, Stocks and Weather.

Gadgets were introduced in Windows Vista, and resided in the Windows Sidebar, on the right of the screen. Windows 7 also supports gadgets, but there's no longer a Sidebar. The gadgets are simply installed to the desktop.

To see the gadgets available and to select gadgets to install:

1 Right-click the desktop and select Gadgets

2 Alternatively, select Start, Control Panel, Appearance and Personalization and click Desktop Gadgets

3 The Desktop Gadget Gallery is displayed

Hot tip

Click Show details to see information about the currently selected gadget, at the bottom of the dialog box.

To add a gadget to the desktop:

1 Open the Desktop Gadget Gallery as above and double-click a gadget to add it to the desktop

2 The gadget is added to the right of the screen, but can be relocated using the Drag handle

3 Right-click a gadget and select Close to remove it from the desktop

To find additional gadgets from the Microsoft Gallery:

 Open the Desktop Gadget Gallery and select Get more gadgets online

You can download more gadgets, from the same location where you find extra themes and desktop backgrounds (see page 187).

2 Click Get more desktop gadgets

3 The desktop gadgets available are listed so you can select a category, or search by keyword

Don't forget

You can download more gadgets, from the same location where you find extra themes and desktop backgrounds (see page 187).

Beware

Most of the gadgets will initially have been designed for Windows Vista. However, these should normally run under Windows 7.

Hot tip

Locate a gadget that interests you, click the Download button and Save the file to hard disk. Run the downloaded file to install the gadget on the desktop and in the Desktop Gadget Gallery.

User Accounts

If more than one person uses the computer, each person can have a user account defined by a user name and optional password. There are three different types of accounts:

- Standard Account – this is the account to use for everyday computing. It lets you use most programs that are installed on the computer, but you can't install or uninstall software and hardware, delete files that are required for the computer to work or change settings on the computer that affect other users

- Administrator Account – this provides the most control over the computer, and should only be used when necessary, e.g. to carry out activities not permitted for a standard user account

- Guest Account – this is primarily for people who need temporary access to the computer. People using the guest account can't install software or hardware, change settings or create a password

Create a User Account

1 Select Control Panel, then click Add or Remove User Accounts (found under the User Accounts and Family Safety category)

User Accounts and Family Safety
Add or remove user accounts
Set up parental controls for any user

2 Click the option to Create a new account

3 Type the name you want to give the user account, click an account type and then click Create Account

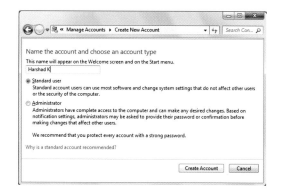

Don't forget

Have two accounts, and use the standard account most of the time, but switch to the administrator account (or use the administrator account password) when administrator permission is required.

4 Select the new account and then click Create a password

Beware

You are always advised to specify a strong password, that contains at least eight characters and a mixture of capital letters, lower case letters, numbers and symbols.

195

5 Enter a password and a hint and click Create password

Hot tip

Since the password is hidden, you are asked to enter it a second time, to confirm. You should also specify a password hint, in case you forget the password for the new account.

Configure the Account

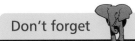

Don't forget

The ability to switch to a different user account without logging off or closing programs and files is called Fast User Switching.

Beware

The Fast User Switching feature is not included in the Starter edition of Windows 7, so you'd need to log off the current account to sign on to the new account.

Hot tip

Click Browse for more pictures to select an image file from your hard disk. For example, you could choose your own photograph.

When you log on to the new account for the first time, your user profile and desktop will be created. You don't necessarily have to shut down the currently active account, you simply switch users.

To switch to the new user account:

1 Click the Start button, click the arrow next to the Lock button and then click Switch User

2 Select the new user name from the Welcome screen

Change the User Account Picture

1 Select Add or Remove User Accounts (see previous page), choose your account and click Change the picture

2 Select a new picture for the account, then scroll down and click Change Picture

Password Reset Disk

You can create a password reset disk to allow you to access your computer and account if you forget your password.

 1 Select Control Panel, User Accounts and Family Safety and User Accounts

 2 Select Create a password reset disk

3 Follow the prompts to create the password reset disk on a floppy drive or a USB drive

4 If you forget your password you can insert this disk, select Reset password and reset the password to a new value

Beware

You need to know the current password to create the disk, but after that anyone with the disk could reset your password. So make sure that you keep the disk safe and secure.

Don't forget

The Forgotten Password wizard adds to the disk a file called userkey.psw which is specific to the particular computer and user account.

Hot tip

The password reset disk will continue to operate, even if you have changed or reset the original password.

Date and Time Functions

To change the format Windows uses to display dates and times:

1 Select Control Panel, click Clock Language and Region, and then click Regional and Language Options

Clock, Language, and Region
Change keyboards or other input methods
Change display language

Region and Language
Install or uninstall display languages
Change display language
Change location
Change the date, time, or number format
Change keyboards or other input methods

2 The Formats tab shows how various data items are displayed

198

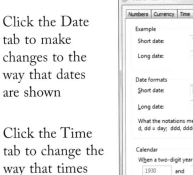

3 Select a different locale, e.g. United Kingdom or Australia, as appropriate

4 Click Additional settings in order to customize the format

5 Click the Date tab to make changes to the way that dates are shown

6 Click the Time tab to change the way that times are displayed

...cont'd

In Windows Live Mail you can create and manage a primary calendar plus extra calendars, such as Birthdays and Festivals, to help you keep track of different types of events.

 1 Open Windows Live Mail and click the Calendar button

Don't forget

The Windows Calendar application found in Windows Vista has been replaced for Windows 7 by the Calendar in Windows Live Mail.

Hot tip

Click Print on the toolbar, and specify a date range to print your calendar by day, week or month.

2 Select the Day, Week or Month button to change the calendar view

3 Click Add Calendar to create extra calendars, specifying the name and the color

 4 Select a date from the Calendar and click the New button to add details for an event, such as subject, location and times, then click Save & close

Don't forget

If you have a Windows Live ID, you can have an online calendar that can be shared with other Windows Live users.

Ease of Access Center

Hot tip

You could also select Start, Control Panel, then Appearance and Personalization, and click Ease of Access Center

Ease of Access Center
Accommodate low vision
Use screen reader
Turn on easy access keys
Turn High Contrast on or off

1 Open Personalization and select Ease of Access Center

Ease of Access Center

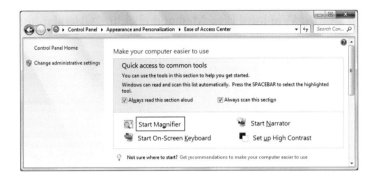

Don't forget

Windows will read and scan the list of common tools. Press the Spacebar to select the currently highlighted tool.

2 Click the bar to get recommendations on the settings that will be most appropriate for you

Don't forget

The Ease of Access Center allows you to turn on and set up programs and settings that make it easier to see your computer and use your mouse and keyboard.

3 Otherwise, scroll down to explore all the settings. Those you select are started automatically each time you log on

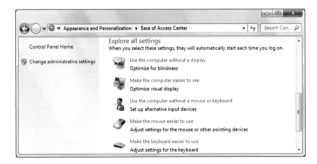

For example, to use the Magnifier:

1 Open the Ease of Access Center and select Magnifier (or press the Spacebar while Magnifier is highlighted)

2 Click the Views button on the Magnifier toolbar to choose Full screen, Lens or Docked operation

Hot tip

Move the mouse pointer over the Magnifying Glass and click it to display the Magnifier toolbar.

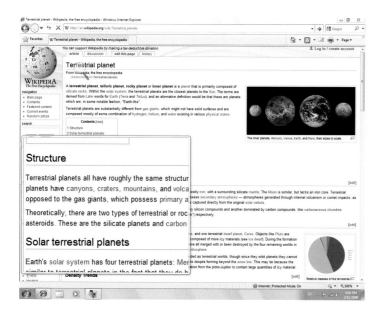

3 Click the Options button on the toolbar to specify the size of the Lens area, or to specify the tracking options for the other modes of operation

4 Click on "Control whether Magnifier starts when I log on" to turn on Magnifier at start up

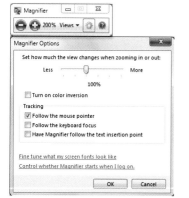

Don't forget

To stop using Magnifier during the session, right-click the taskbar icon and select Close Window.

Mouse Settings

1 Open Personalization and select Change mouse pointers to display Mouse Properties

2 The Pointers tab should be selected. Click the Scheme bar to select a mouse pointer scheme, including large and extra large pointers

3 Click the Pointer Options tab to Adjust the pointer speed, faster or slower or to choose Snap To to have the pointer move to the default button in a dialog box

Hot tip

You can make the pointer easier to find if you choose to display pointer trails, or choose to Show location of pointer when you press the Ctrl key.

4 Select the Buttons tab to Switch left and right button functions, or to test and adjust the Double-click speed

Don't forget

Select the Wheel tab to specify the scrolling increment for the wheel on a wheel mouse.

11 Digital Media

Windows 7 and Windows Live Essentials make it easy to work with digital media, to organize your collections of pictures, videos and music files, create your own CDs and DVDs and use your PC as a media center.

204 Upload Pictures

206 Windows Live Photo Gallery

208 Windows Live Movie Maker

210 Windows DVD Maker

212 Windows Media Player

213 Copy Audio CD

214 Play DVD Movies

215 Media Library

216 Online Resources

217 Windows Media Center

Upload Pictures

Windows makes it easy to transfer pictures from digital media, camera or scanner. Here's an example using a media card reader.

1 Plug the reader into a USB port on the computer and insert the memory card with the photos you want to view

2 The first time you do this, the New Hardware Wizard will identify and install the device driver software required

Installing device driver software ⚹ ✕
Click here for status.

Your device is ready to use ⚹ ✕
Device driver software installed successfully.

3 A drive letter is assigned and AutoPlay lists your options

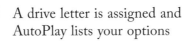

Removable Disk (F:)

3.18 GB free of 3.78 GB

Hot tip

You can import the pictures using the Windows Photo Viewer, and import or view using the Windows Live Photo Gallery (if you have installed the Windows Live Essentials).

4 Select Open folder to view files to explore the contents

5 Open folders and subfolders as required to view pictures stored on the memory card

Hot tip

Use the Preview pane (see page 76) for folders containing pictures, to see a larger version of the selected thumbnail or file icon.

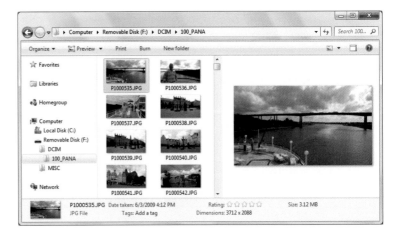

...cont'd

You can use Windows Photo Viewer to explore the pictures in the form of a slide show:

 Click the Preview button on the toolbar

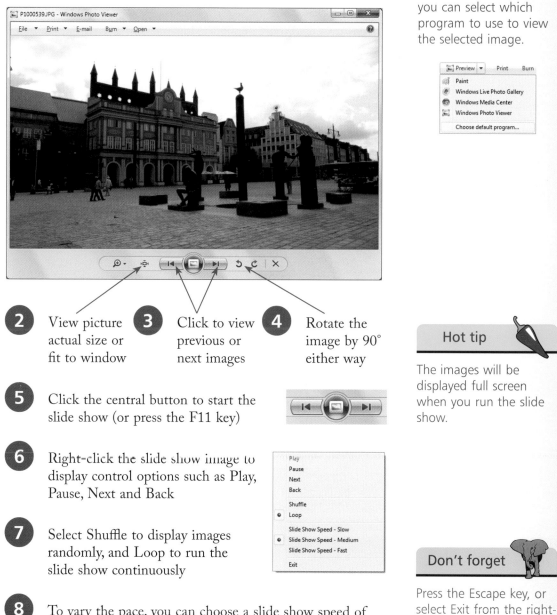

2 View picture actual size or fit to window

3 Click to view previous or next images

4 Rotate the image by 90° either way

5 Click the central button to start the slide show (or press the F11 key)

6 Right-click the slide show image to display control options such as Play, Pause, Next and Back

7 Select Shuffle to display images randomly, and Loop to run the slide show continuously

8 To vary the pace, you can choose a slide show speed of Slow, Medium or Fast

Hot tip

Click the arrow next to the Preview button, and you can select which program to use to view the selected image.

Preview ▾ Print Burn
- Paint
- Windows Live Photo Gallery
- Windows Media Center
- Windows Photo Viewer
- Choose default program...

Hot tip

The images will be displayed full screen when you run the slide show.

Don't forget

Press the Escape key, or select Exit from the right-click menu, to end the slide show.

Windows Live Photo Gallery

1 Connect your digital camera or media card reader and Windows detects the picture files and lists suitable actions

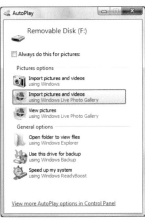

Windows detects your newest pictures, and does not import duplicates of pictures that you have previously copied to your computer.

2 Select Import pictures using Windows Live Photo Gallery

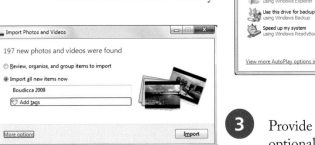

3 Provide name and optionally a tag

Beware

Portrait style photos will be automatically rotated. Click More Options to amend this and other settings used during the import process.

4 Click Import and your photos will be copied to the hard disk and displayed on screen

5 Hold the mouse pointer over an image to see it enlarged

Hot tip

The files on the camera or media card are copied to a subfolder in the Pictures folder (using the name provided), and Windows Live Photo Gallery opens with that folder selected.

...cont'd

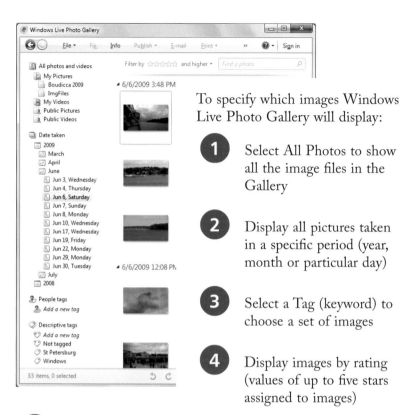

To specify which images Windows Live Photo Gallery will display:

1 Select All Photos to show all the image files in the Gallery

2 Display all pictures taken in a specific period (year, month or particular day)

3 Select a Tag (keyword) to choose a set of images

4 Display images by rating (values of up to five stars assigned to images)

5 Double-click an image file to see it enlarged, and click the Info button for image details

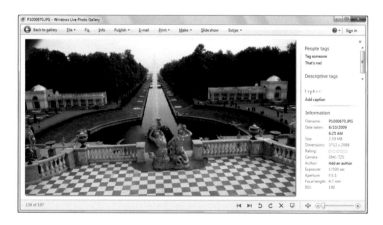

6 The Previous, Next, Rotate, Slide Show, Size and Zoom buttons at the bottom allow you to control the view

Don't forget

Windows Live Photo Gallery allows you to view and organize all the pictures stored in your Pictures folder and subfolders, the public Pictures, and any other image folders you add to the Gallery.

Don't forget

Click Fix and Auto Adjust your photos, or apply individual changes such as exposure, color, photo straightening, size and red eye removal.

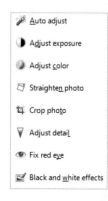

Windows Live Movie Maker

You use Windows Live Movie Maker to obtain audio and video clips from a digital video camera, then use this captured content in your movies. You can also import existing audio, video or still pictures to incorporate in your movies.

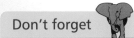
1 Select Start, All Programs and Windows Live, and then click Windows Live Movie Maker

2 Movie Maker warns you if there are problems with your graphics card support for required features e.g. DirectX9

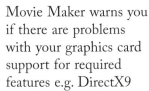

3 Click the Import Media button to select your video clips and still photos, and then click the Import button

4 Problem files are identified, and you can fix them or remove them

5 Drag and drop the video clips and photos to assemble them in the sequence needed for your movie

6 Add soundtracks to associate with particular clips or stills

7 Click Animations or Visual Effects to add various effects

8 Click Edit to adjust text and durations and trim clips

9 Select a Sharing option to publish your movie on the web, to write it to DVD or to create a video file

Windows DVD Maker

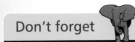
Don't forget

The video discs run in a DVD player so you can watch your movies and slide shows on your TV.

You can create DVD-Video discs using Windows DVD Maker, adding video, pictures and audio to make slide shows. You can also add projects created using Movie Maker. To create a DVD:

 Insert a blank DVD into your DVD writer

 Select Burn a DVD Video disc using Windows DVD Maker

 The first time, you'll see an initial welcome screen. Make sure that the Don't show this Page Again box is ticked

Hot tip

If you don't select the AutoPlay option, you can select Start, All Programs, Windows DVD Maker.

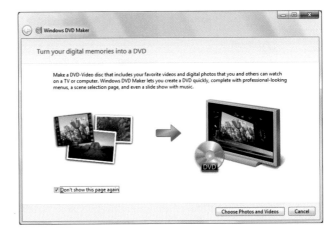

 Click Choose Pictures and Videos to open the project

Hot tip

By default, Windows DVD Maker will enter the current date as the disc title for the project, but you can append this or enter a new title.

 Specify the disc title if desired, then click the Add Items button to select your pictures and videos

Hot tip

Click Ctrl+A to highlight all the entries in the current folder and add them to your DVD project.

 Add movies, video clips or still images and photographs

Hot tip

Click Options to change settings such as the aspect ratio (4:3 or 16:9) and the video format (NTSC or PAL).

211

 When you've added all the items, click Next

Don't forget

Click the Preview button to check out the film show before you commit to writing it to disc.

Preview your DVD

8 Click the Burn button to write the project to the DVD

Windows Media Player

The Windows Media Player will manage audio and video digital media files, allowing you to copy music files, organize your collections, download media files etc.

If the Autoplay option isn't set, click Play audio CD using Windows Media Player. Click the box to make this the default action.

 To play an audio CD, insert the disc into the CD drive

2 Windows Media Player starts up and begins playing the CD from track one, initially with no disc details

3 If you are connected to the Internet, the artist, album title and track details are automatically downloaded and saved

4 Right-click the Title bar area and select Show List, and the details for the tracks on the CD are displayed

When you move the mouse over the Media Player window, the playback controls appear.

212

5 Double-click any track to start playing at that point

Copy Audio CD

You can rip (copy) tracks from your audio CDs, so that they are stored as digital files, based on the settings.

1 Right-click the Title bar area and select More options from the menu displayed

2 Choose the location to store files

3 Select the format, e.g. .wma, .mp3 or .wav

4 Specify the quality that you require

5 Click OK then click the Start Rip button to start copying

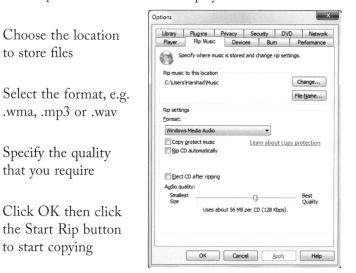

6 The tracks are extracted while the music plays, and the status is shown by the changes in the Rip button icon

Ready to Rip   Rip in Process   Already Ripped

7 The album folder is added to the artist's folder in Music

Hot tip

By default, the files will be stored as a subfolder within the user's own Music folder, under the artist's name.

Beware

Copy protection is available for Windows Media Audio (.wma) format. However, if you intend to use the digital audio files on more than one computer, do not copy protect the files.

Don't forget

You'll now be able to start Media Player and play all the music that you have copied to your system.

213

Play DVD Movies

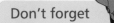

Don't forget

To play DVDs you must have a DVD drive and a compatible DVD decoder, provided with all editions of Windows 7 except Home Basic and Starter (with these you download a Windows Media Player add-in to support DVD playback).

Hot tip

If you stop the movie, right-click the DVD drive in the Computer folder and select Play.

 To play a DVD movie, insert the disc into the drive

 If autoplay isn't set, click Play DVD movie using Windows Media Player

 Windows Media Player starts up and begins playing the movie, initially in full screen mode

 Move the mouse, and the playback control tools appear below the movie image

 To switch between full screen and windowed display, press the Full Screen button, or use the Alt+Enter key combination

6 Press the DVD button and select Special Features, to access the extra items on the disc

Media Library

Windows Media Player monitors your personal folders and adds information about the music, video and picture files that they contain or that you add. When you play CDs, the downloaded information about the discs is also added. When you play a digital file on your computer or on the Internet, those details are also added, if not already in the library.

Don't forget

To open Windows Media Player without inserting a CD, select Start, All Programs, Windows Media Player, or click the launch button on the taskbar.

1 To display the library, start the Media Player and click the Switch to Library button

2 The library displays the category that you viewed last, in this case Music. View the contents by artist, album etc

Beware

The Media Player does not automatically add files that you play from removable storage or network drives.

3 To display a different category, click the address bar triangle after Library and choose from the list offered

4 To remove an item in the library, right-click it and select Delete

5 You'll be asked if you want to remove just the library link or to remove the file completely

Don't forget

The library contains links to the digital media files on your computer, it does not have actual copies of the files. These are contained in the Music, Videos and Pictures folders.

Online Resources

You can use Windows Media Player to find and subscribe to music, video, radio services, and other types of content from online stores provided by Internet content providers.

Don't forget

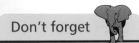

Whichever choice you make, Online Stores or Media Guide, it will be displayed as the default choice until the next time you switch choices.

1 From Media Player Library click the Online Stores button (or if the Media Guide button shows, click the down arrow then click Browse all online stores)

Hot tip

The Media Guide is a live web page or electronic magazine, hosted by WindowsMedia.com. It is updated daily with links to the latest movies, music, and video on the Internet.

2 To view an electronic magazine, click the Media Guide button (or if the Online Stores button shows, click the down arrow then click Media Guide)

Windows Media Center

Windows 7 (other than Starter and Home Basic) offers another way to manage digital media files and play CDs and DVDs, and in addition support TV and FM Radio. To explore this feature:

 1 Select Start, All Programs, Windows Media Center. The first time you do this, you will run the setup program

 2 Select Express to be able to download material from the Internet and to enroll in the customer feedback program

 3 When configuration completes, scroll to the Music section to begin cataloging your multimedia files

Hot tip

Select Learn More to go online and find out how to get the most from Windows Media Center.

Don't forget

Select Custom to set up Windows Media Center step by step, choosing your preferred settings.

...cont'd

4 Windows Media Center will locate and identify your music files and set up your music library

5 Scroll to the Online Media section to explore its options, which include TV, movies, music, news and sport

6 For example, select the Showcase option and select Arsenal TV to watch games or view greatest moments etc

12 System and Security

Windows includes a set of
tools to enhance the security,
performance and reliability
of your PC. It helps you to
maintain your hard drive at
peak efficiency, protects your
computer from malicious
software and keeps your
system up to date.

220 System Properties

222 Performance Information

223 Clean Up Your Disk

225 Back Up and Recover Data

226 System Restore

228 Action Center

229 Windows Firewall

230 Malware Protection

231 Windows Update

232 Change Settings

System Properties

There are several ways to open the System Properties, and view information about your computer:

1 Select Start, Control Panel, System and Security and then click the System category

2 Select Start, type *system*, and select the Control Panel System entry displayed

3 Press the Windows Logo + the Pause/Break keys

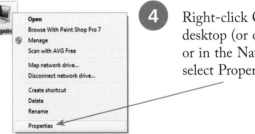

4 Right-click Computer on the desktop (or on the Start menu, or in the Navigation pane) and select Properties from the menu

Control Panel ▸ System and Security ▸ System

Search Con...

View basic information about your computer

Windows edition

Windows 7 Ultimate

Copyright © 2009 Microsoft Corporation. All rights reserved.

Control Panel Home
Device Manager
Remote settings
System protection
Advanced system settings

System

Rating: Windows Experience Index
Processor: Intel(R) Core(TM)2 CPU   6400 @ 2.13GHz 2.13 GHz
Installed memory (RAM): 4.00 GB (3.00 GB usable)
System type: 32-bit Operating System
Pen and Touch: No Pen or Touch Input is available for this Display

Computer name, domain, and workgroup settings

Computer name: Harshad-PC
Full computer name: Harshad-PC
Computer description:
Workgroup: WORKGROUP

Change settings

Windows activation

Windows is activated
Product ID: 11112-221-2222222-11112   Change product key

genuine
Microsoft software

See also
Action Center
Windows Update
Performance Information and Tools

Learn more online...

Device Manager

1 Click Device Manager, to list all of the hardware components that are installed on your computer

2 Click the ▷ symbol to expand that entry to show details

3 Click the ◢ symbol to collapse the expanded entry

4 Double-click any device to open its properties

5 Select the Drivers tab and click Update Driver to find and install new software

6 Select Disable to put the particular device offline. The button changes to Enable, to reverse the action

Don't forget

You may be prompted for an administrator password or asked for permission to continue, when you select some Device Manager entries.

221

Hot tip

Click the Roll Back Driver button to switch back to the previously installed driver for that device, if the new one fails.

Performance Information

The System Properties panel displays the Windows Experience Index, the overall capability of your system. To view the details:

 Open System Properties and click Performance Information and Tools. Typical results for an Aero capable PC are:

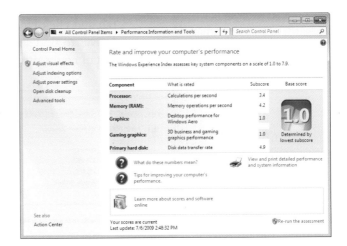

 Typical results for a Windows 7 Basic system are:

3 If you upgrade any of the hardware components on your computer click Re-run the Assessment to see the effect

Clean Up Your Disk

1 Select Performance Information and Tools and click Start Disk Cleanup

2 Select the drive letter, if there's more than one drive available

Hot tip

You can select Start, All Programs, Accessories, System Tools, Disk Cleanup. You can also select Start, type *Disk Cleanup* and select the program from the top of the Start menu.

3 Drive Cleanup scans the drive to identify files that can be safely removed

4 All the possible files are listed by category, and the sets of files recommended to be deleted are marked with a tick symbol

Don't forget

You can have more than one hard disk on your computer, or you can divide one hard disk into several partitions, with separate drive letters.

223

5 Make changes to the selections, clicking View Files if necessary to help you choose

Beware

You can select any of the groups of files listed, but this could affect the operation of some functions, for example, hibernate.

6 Click the button to Clean up system files, to include these also, then click OK

7 Deleted files won't be transferred to the Recycle Bin, so confirm that you do want to permanently delete all of these files. The files will be removed and the disk space will become available

...cont'd

When a file is written to the hard disk, it may be stored in several pieces in different places. This fragmentation of disk space can slow down your computer. Disk Defragmenter rearranges the data so the disk will work more efficiently.

1 Select Start, type *Defrag* and click Disk Defragmenter at the top of the Start menu

2 The program runs as a scheduled task, but you can select a drive and click Analyze disk to check out a new drive

3 Click Defragment disk to process the selected disk. This may take from several minutes to several hours to complete, depending on the size and state of the disk, but you can still use your computer while the task is running

Back Up and Recover Data

1 Open Control Panel and click Back up your computer, in the System and Security category

 System and Security
Review your computer's status
Back up your computer
Find and fix problems

2 The first time you do this, you must select Set up backup

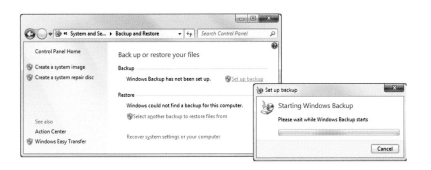

3 Choose where you want to save your backup – an external hard disk is recommended or you can use a network drive

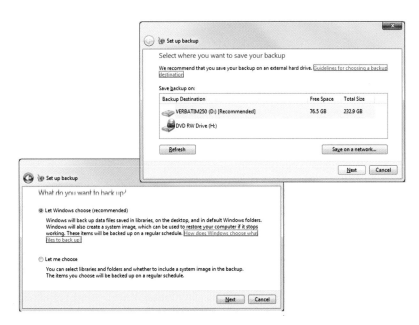

4 Let Windows choose what to back up, or choose the files yourself, then follow the prompts to set up the backup

Don't forget

To make sure you don't lose the files stored on your computer, you should back them up regularly. Windows will help you set up automatic backups.

Beware

The ability to back up to network drives is not included in Windows 7 Starter or Home editions.

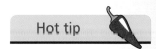

Hot tip

You can create a system image and also back up data files in the libraries and other folders on your system.

225

System Restore

Hot tip
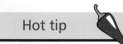

System Restore returns system files to an earlier point in time, allowing you to undo system changes without affecting your documents, email, and other data files.

Windows takes snapshots of the system files before any software updates are applied, or in any event once every seven days. You can also create a snapshot manually. The snapshots are known as Restore Points and are managed by System Restore.

1 Open System Properties (see page 220) and select System Protection

2 Click the Create button, to create a restore point manually

3 Provide a title for the restore point and click Create

4 The required data is written to disk and the manual restore point is set up

Beware

System Restore is not intended for protecting personal data files. For these you should use the Windows Backup program (see page 225).

Using Restore Points

The installation of a new program or driver software may make Windows behave unpredictably or have other unexpected results. Usually, uninstalling the program or rolling back the driver (see page 221) will correct the situation. If this does not fix the problem, you use an automatic or manual restore point to reset your system to an earlier date when everything worked correctly.

1 Select System Protection and click the System Restore button

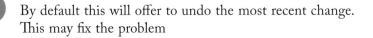

2 By default this will offer to undo the most recent change. This may fix the problem

3 Otherwise, click Choose a different restore point, and pick a suitable time

4 Follow the prompts to restart the system using system files from the selected date and time

Hot tip

You can also select Start, All Programs, Accessories, System tools and then select System Restore.

 System Restore

Don't forget

You can also run System Restore from Safe Mode, the troubleshooting option. Start up the computer and press F8 repeatedly as your computer reboots, to display the boot menu, then select Safe Mode.

Don't forget

If the selected restore point does not resolve the problem, you can try again, selecting another restore point.

Action Center

The Action Center monitors security and system maintenance issues and delivers alerts for features such as Windows Backup.

 Move the mouse over the Action Center icon in the system tray to see the status. If a problem is detected, the icon is marked with a red cross

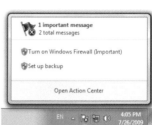

2 Click the icon for more details, then select Open Action Center

 You can solve the problems from the Action Center, or click Change Action Center Settings to adjust the alerts

Windows Firewall

1 Open Control Panel, select the System and Security category and click Windows Firewall

2 Click Turn Windows Firewall on or off to customize settings for private (home and work) and public networks

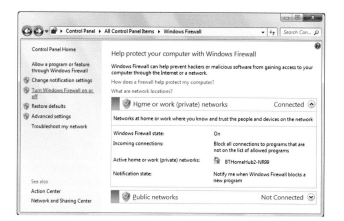

3 Click Allow a program or feature through Windows Firewall, to view the allowed programs

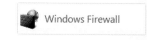

4 Click Allow another program, if you need to Add a program

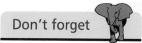

229

Malware Protection

Don't forget

Malware (malicious software) is designed to deliberately harm your computer. To protect your system, you need up to date antivirus and antispyware software. Windows Defender provides the latter, but you must install a separate antivirus program (see page 36).

Hot tip

You can also click the Windows Defender button in Control Panel, View by Icon.

Beware

The default scan time is 2 am. If the computer is normally switched off before then, you'll never get a scan. Make sure to choose a practical schedule time.

1 Open Control Panel, type *Defender* in the Search box and select Windows Defender

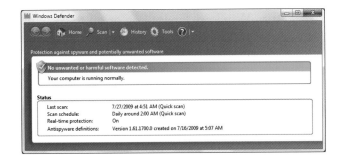

2 Click Tools, then select Options and adjust settings such as automatic scanning and default actions

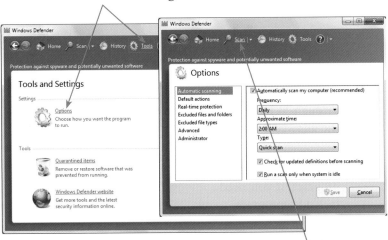

3 For an immediate check, click Scan from Windows Defender, or Scan now from an Action Center alert

Windows Update

Windows Update manages updates to Windows and other
Microsoft products. Applying updates can prevent or fix problems,
improve the security or enhance performance, so Windows
Update can be set up to install important updates automatically.
To review your settings for Windows Update:

Hot tip

Alternatively, you can
click Windows Update
from Action Center, or
select Start, All Programs
and then click Windows
Update.

1 Select Control Panel, System
and Security and then click
Windows Update (or select Windows
Update in Control Panel, View by Icons)

Don't forget

Click View update history
to see the changes that
have previously been
applied to your system.

2 To see if there are any updates that are waiting to be
downloaded and applied, click Check for Updates

3 If there are updates, click Install updates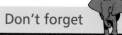
to download and apply them immediately, or wait for
Windows Update to install them at the scheduled time

231

Change Settings

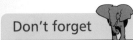

Don't forget

Updates for Windows and other Microsoft products are provided free of charge, other than any telephone and Internet service charges that may apply to your connection.

1 Open Windows Update and click Change settings

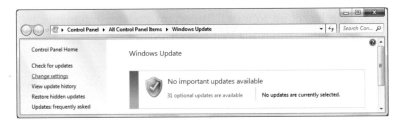

2 The recommended option is to install updates automatically. This assumes a broadband link

Hot tip

By default Windows will include recommended updates, or you can clear the box to restrict the process to critical updates only.

3 You can specify to download updates in the background, but pick your own time to install them

Install updates automatically (recommended)
Download updates but let me choose whether to install them
Check for updates but let me choose whether to download and install them
Never check for updates (not recommended)

Beware

You may need to turn off Windows Update completely, by choosing Never check for updates, when you are traveling where the Internet connections available are unsuitable for downloading.

4 Alternatively, you can have Windows Update check for updates and alert you when they are available, but choose for yourself when to both download and install them

Index

Symbols

32-bit processor	12–13
3D Flip	59
64-bit processor	10, 12–13

A

Action Center	36–37, 121, 228
Activation	19, 41
Add-ons	134, 138, 139
Add a printer	42
Address bar	50, 66, 74–75, 138
Address bar searches	140
Add to compressed folder	105
Add to favorites	138
Add to library	72
Adjacent block	86
Adjust photographs	207
Administrative tools	22
Administrator	23, 28, 194
Adobe Reader	66
Advanced boot options	22
Aero	12, 30
Aero Peek	30, 55
Aero Snaps	56
Aero Themes	30, 183
Get more themes	187
All files and folders	87
All Programs	31, 35, 68, 110
Alternative programs	102
Always show menus	49
Antivirus protection	36–37
Appearance and Personalization	182
Arrange icons	60
Arrange windows	54
Ask button	40
Associated programs	102
Attachments	150
Autoplay	91, 212
AVG antivirus software	37

B

Back	39, 50, 138
Backtrack file operations	100
Back up	225
Backup files and folders	93
Basic	12, 30, 188
Bing	135, 140
BitLocker drive encryption	12
Block spam senders	164
Bookmark Favorites	142
Broadband connection	132
Browser buttons	138
Browse the web	136
Browsing history	144
Burn to disc	65, 91
Bypass the Recycle Bin	97

C

Cable connection	132
Calculator	48
Cascade windows	54
Change search provider	141
Change user account picture	196
Changing views	78
Character Map	108
Check box	49
Check for updates	231
Classic	12
Clean Install	14
Clean up your disk	223 224
Clear recent items	103
Close program	110–111
Close window	52, 62
Collapse	67
Color scheme	184–185
Command bar	65, 139
Command button	49
Command Prompt	126
Open as administrator	127
Compare windows	57
Compatibility	9, 121, 123–124
Compose message	158
Compressed folders	105

Compressed item properties	106
Computer	60, 64–65, 220
Configure user account	196
Configure XP Mode	124
Conflicts with files and folders	92
Connect to the Internet	133
Contacts	75
Context menu	26
Control icon	50–51
Control menu	51, 62
Control Menu Move	51
Control Menu Size	53
Control Panel	26, 75, 83, 220
Administrative tools	22
View by Icons	119
Copy a character	108
Copy audio CD	213
Copy files and folders	88
Create compressed folder	105
Create files and folders	98
Create new Library	71
Create shortcut	113
Create user account	28, 194–195
Currency symbol	19
Customize folders	84
Customize layout	76
Customize library	72
Cut, Copy, Paste files and folders	90

Disk Cleanup	223–224
Disk defragmenter	224
Display a web page	137
Display menu bar	48
Display settings	191
Documents	31, 48, 64, 74, 77, 104
Double-click	24
Drag files and folders	89
Dragging	24
Dual Boot	14
DVD-RW optical drive	12
DVD-Video disc	210

E

Ease of Access Center	26, 200–201
Magnifier	201
On-Screen keyboard	26
Recommendations	200
Eject button	65
Email servers	154
Enable Pop Mail	152
Ethernet	168
Expand	67, 69
Explore drive	66
Explorer. See Windows Explorer	
Extract files and folders	106

D

Date and time functions	198–199
Deactivate Recycle Bin	97
Delete files and folders	94
Delete shortcut	113
Desktop	30, 75
Desktop background	183
Desktop Gadgets	192–193
Desktop icons	60, 189
Details pane	50, 66
Details view	79
Device Manager	221
Devices and Printers	42
Dial-up connection	132
Dialog box	49
Digital media resources	216
Digital media upload	204
Digital Subscriber Line (DSL)	132
Dimmed option	48
Discover networks	172

F

Fast user switching	10, 46
Favorites	67, 69, 138
Favorites Center	144
File Properties	101
Files and folders	
Backup	93
Burn to Disc	91
Conflicts	92
Copy	88
Create	98
Create shortcut	113
Cut, Copy, Paste	90
Delete	94
Delete shortcut	113
Drag	89

Move	88
Rename	99
Search	104
Select	86–87
Share	179
File type	98
Filtering	80
Finalize settings	21
Find a character	108
Find a program online	36
Fix photographs	207
Flip 3D	59
Folder contents	77
Folder Options	49, 82–83
Folders on Taskbar	115
Font samples	107
Fonts Folder	107
Forward	39, 50

G

Gadget Gallery	192–193
Gadgets	55, 192–193
Games	76
Genuine copy of Windows	41
Gestures	25
Getting Started	32
Gmail	152
Google	141
Graphical User Interface (GUI)	8
Graphics adapter	12
Graphics memory	12
Greyed option	48
Group By	60, 81
Group task buttons	58, 64
Guest	46, 194

H

Hard disk drive	65
Hardware power button	45
Help and Support Center	38–39
Hibernate	44
Hide file extensions	98
Hide menu bar	48

History	144
Home Basic. *See* Windows 7: Home Basic	
HomeGroup	20, 67, 172
Join	174–175
Sharing	179
Home network	20
Home page	145
Home Premium. *See* Windows 7: Home Premium	
HP TouchSmart	25
Hyperlink	137

I

Icon size	77
IM invitation	160
IM status	160
Include in library	70
Insert a character	108
Installation options	14
Install program	119
Install router	170
Instant messaging (IM)	160
Internet connection	132, 170
Internet Explorer	75
Address bar	138
Add to Favorites	138
Bookmark Favorites	142
Browser buttons	138
Browse the Web	136
Browsing History	144
Change search provider	141
Command bar	139
Custom settings	135
Display a web page	137
Express settings	135
Favorites	138
Favorites Center	144
History	144
Home Page	145
Hyperlink	137
Manage add-ons	139
No add-ons	134
Print	148
Quick Tabs	138, 146
Reset home page	145
RSS Feeds	143
Search box	138
Search engine	135
Search the Internet	140
Send web page	166

Start	134
Suggested sites	134
Tabbed browsing	146
Tab List	138
View Favorites	142
Web Mail	150
Web slices	143
Zoom	147
Internet Service Provider (ISP)	132

Jump List	62, 64, 103

Keyboard zoom	147

Layout	76
Left mouse button	24
Libraries	31, 67, 70–71, 73, 79
Arrange by	71
Properties	101
Save location	73
Library location	70
Live preview	58, 64
Location	65, 72, 74
Lock	44
Logoff	44

Magnifier	201

Malware protection	23, 230
Manage add-ons	139
Map network	177
Maximize	50, 51
Media Library	215
Menu bar	48, 50, 76
Message header	151
Message icons	156
Microsoft Office	13
Microsoft Windows. *See* Windows	
Millennium	8
Minimize	50
More assistance	38, 40
Most recently used programs	110
Mouse	24
Mouse button	61
Mouse pointer	50, 202
Mouse settings	202
Mouse wheel	24–25, 61
Move files and folders	88
Move window	51
MS-DOS	8
MSN Hotmail	35
MSN Music	35
Multilingual User Interface (MUI)	10
Multimonitor support	10, 51
Multitouch	25
Multitouch keyboard	26
Music	31, 64, 77
My Computer	65
My Documents	31

Navigation pane	65, 67, 69, 73, 82, 220
Network	67
Components	168
Discover networks	172
HomeGroup	172
Install hardware	169
Install router	170
Internet connection	170
Location	172
Map	177
Setup	169
Share files and folders	179
Sharing printer	176
Troubleshooting	180
View components	178
Network and Sharing Center	132, 173

Network map	177
Open	174
Troubleshoot	180
View components	178
Networked drive	65
Network location	20, 172
Network status	132
Newsgroups	162
Subscribe	163
New York Times	141
Non-adjacent files	87
Notepad	48, 64

O

OEM system	10
Office network	20
On-Screen keyboard	26
Online Help	39
Online media	218
On-screen power button	45
Open Files	102
OpenType	107
Open window	54, 62
Optical mouse	24
Organize	76, 82

P

Page setup	43
Paint	48
Paperclip	150
Password	18, 195
Password hint	29
Password reset disk	28, 197
PC Requirements	12
Performance information	222
Permanently erase files	96
Permission	23
Personalize Windows	32, 64, 182
Aero Themes	183
Color scheme	184–185
Desktop Background	183
Desktop icons	189
Get more themes	187

Screen Saver	186
Sound scheme	184–185
Transparency	184
Phishing	164
Physical power button	45
Pictures	31, 64, 77
Pin to Start menu	114, 134
Pin to Taskbar	115
Play audio CD	212
Play DVD movies	214
Pop Mail	
Enable	152
Windows Live Mail	151
Power button	45
Power options	45
Pre-install	14
Preserve File Types	99
Preview window	58
Print	43
Print preview	43, 148
Print web page	148
Product key	19
Professional. See Windows 7: Professional	
Program	
Close	110–111
Install	119
Start	110
Uninstall	119
Program compatibility	9, 121, 123–124
Public network	20

Q

Quick Launch Bar	30
Quick Tabs	138, 146

R

Radio button	49
Receive emails	155
Recent items	103
Recently used programs	31–32
Recover data	225
Recovery partition	22
Recycle Bin	75, 95, 223

Bypass	97
Deactivate	97
Empty	96
Permanently erase files	96
Resize	97
Restoring files	95
Redo	100
Registry editor	23
Remove location	72
Rename Files and Folders	99
Reply to message	157
Reset home page	145
Reset password	29, 197
Resize Recycle Bin	97
Resize window	53
Resource Monitor	130
Restart	44
Restore defaults	83
Restore point	226
Restore window	50, 52, 57
Reveal file extensions	98
Rich Text File	98
Right mouse button	24
RSS Feeds	143
Ruler	50

S

Safe Mode	227
Save your work	62
Scenic Ribbon	48, 50
Screen resolution	64, 190
Screen Saver	186
Scroll arrows	24
Scroll bar	50, 61
Scroll box	61
Scrolling	61
Search	
Character map	108
Files and folders	104
Help	39–40
Internet	140, 204
Provider	35, 138–139, 141
Start menu	31, 112
Search box	50, 65, 138, 230
Security software providers	36
Select Files and Folders	86
Select user	28
Send web page	166
Sequential Files	86

Service Set Identifier (SSI)	171
Share files and folders	179
Share printer	176
Shortcut keys	48, 56, 62, 90
Show all folders	67
Show desktop	25, 30, 55
Show desktop icons	55, 189
Shutdown	44
Side by Side windows	54
Sign on	28
Single-click	24
Sleep	44–45
Slider	61
SmartScreen filter	164
Sort By option	81
Sorting files	79
Sound scheme	184–185
Spam	150
Block senders	164
Spin box	49
Spyware	23
Stack windows	54
Standard user	23, 194
Start button	30–31, 65, 68, 110
Starter. See Windows 7: Starter	
Starting Windows 7	18–19, 28
Start Internet Explorer	134
Start maximized	118
Start menu	64, 110
Properties	49
Start menu search	112
Start minimized	118
Start program	110
Startup	117
Status bar	50
Structure of window	50
Subfolders	77
Suggested Sites	134
Switch users	10, 44, 46
Switch windows	58
System partition	22
System properties	220
Device Manager	221
Performance information	222
System Recovery Environment	22
System Restore	226–227

T

Tabbed browsing	146

Tab list   138
Tabs   49
Taskbar   30, 55
Taskbar grouping   116
Task button   30, 52, 64
Task Manager
    Performance   129
    Processes   128
Tile windows   54
Time and date functions   198–199
Time zone   19
Title bar   50
Transparency   51, 184
Troubleshooting   180
TrueType   107
Turn off your computer   44

U

Ultimate. See Windows 7: Ultimate
Undo   54, 100
Ungroup task buttons   58, 116
Uniform Resource Locator (URL)   136
Uninstall program   119
Unpin from Start menu   114
Upgrade   14
Upgrade Advisor   12, 15
    Reports   16
    Windows XP   17
Upgrade Option program   14
Upgrade reports   16
Upload pictures   204
USB   45
USB device   15, 65, 66
USB flash drive   29
USB printer   42
User Account
    Change picture   196
User account   18
    Add   196
    Configure   196
    Password reset disk   197
    Remove   196
User Account Control (UAC)   23
User Accounts   194
Using restore points   226
Using your mouse   24, 38

V

Videos   77
View available fonts   107
View Favorites   142
View menu   48
View network components   178
View Newsgroups   162
View update history   231
Vista   8, 79
Volume licensing   10

W

Web address   136
Web Mail   150
    Message header   151
Web slices   143
Welcome Center   30, 32
Welcome screen   28
Wheel mouse   24, 25
Wheel mouse zoom   147
Wikipedia   141
Windows   8
    Editions   9–11
    Versions   8–9
Windows 2000   14
Windows 7   9
    Activation   19, 41
    Antivirus protection   36–37
    Enterprise   10
    Features   11
    Graphics adapter   12
    Graphics memory   12
    Help and Support Center   38–39
    Home Basic   10
    HomeGroup   20
    Home Premium   9
    Installation options   14
    PC Requirements   12, 15
    Personalization   32
    Prices   14
    Product key   19
    Professional   9
    Retail editions   9
    Security software providers   36
    Starter   9, 10
    Starting   18, 28

System Recovery Environment	22
Ultimate	9
XP Mode	12, 123
Windows 7 Basic	188, 222
Windows 7 Upgrade Advisor. *See* Upgrade Advisor	
Windows Anytime Upgrade	9, 14
Windows Defender	230
Windows DVD Maker	210
Add clips	211
Burn	211
Windows Explorer	64, 84
Close	80
Open	68
Organize	76
Windows features	
Turn on or off	120
Windows Firewall	229
Windows Flip	59
Windows Gadgets	192–193
Windows Live Contacts	159
Windows Live Essentials	33–34
Windows Live ID	35, 160
Windows Live Mail	150, 151, 152
Calendar	199
Compose message	158
Contacts	159
Junk email	165
Message icons	156
Newsgroups	162
Receive emails	155
Reply to message	157
Safe Senders List	165
Send web page	166
Start	153
Windows Live Messenger	35, 160
Add contact	161
Windows Live Movie Maker	
Add clips	209
Import	208
Windows Live Photo Gallery	
Import	206
Organize pictures	207
Rotate	206
Windows Live Search. *See* Bing	
Windows Live settings	35
Windows logo key	31, 42, 46, 112
Windows Mail	33, 152
Windows Media Audio (wma)	213
Windows Media Center	9, 217
Music library	218
Online media	218
Setup	217
Windows Media Player	10, 64, 178, 212
Copy audio CD	213
Media Library	215

Online resources	216
play audio CD	212
Play DVD movies	214
Windows Movie Maker	33
Windows Photo Gallery	33
Windows Photo Viewer	204
Preview	205
Windows Recovery	22
Windows Remote Assistance	40
Windows structure	50
Windows Touch	25–26
Windows Update	17, 19, 231
Change settings	232
View update history	231
Windows Upgrade Option program	14
Windows Virtual PC	12, 122–123
Windows Vista. *See* Vista	
Windows XP. *See* XP	
Wireless	171
Wireless network	20, 133, 168
WordPad	48, 50, 64, 103, 110

X

XP	8, 14, 17
XP Mode. *See* Windows 7: XP Mode	

Z

Zoom	25, 147